UNSUNG HERO

Margaret Allyn Greene Best

MARGARET ALLYN GREENE BEST

UNSUNG HERO

THE LIFE AND TIMES OF ALBERT V. GREENE
A BIOGRAPHY

AS TOLD BY
MARGARET ALLYN GREENE BEST

INCLUDING

WORLD WAR II EXPERIENCES
OF ALBERT V. GREENE

A MEMOIR
WRITTEN BY
ALBERT V. GREENE

ISBN: 978-1-4834-7908-8 (sc)
ISBN: 978-1-4834-7910-1 (hc)
ISBN: 978-1-4834-7909-5 (e)

Library of Congress Control Number: 2018900224

Lulu Publishing Services rev. date: 01/22/2018

To the many service members and their
families whose stories were never told.

CONTENTS

ACKNOWLEDGMENTS

This book would have never seen the light of day if my father, Albert Vincent Greene, had not written his World War II memoir at our request.

> "I've had quite a life," he said to me.
> "Yes, Dad. So when are you going to write about it?"
> "I'm not finished living it yet."

A special thank-you goes to him for writing at least part of his story. I also wish to acknowledge the help that my brother, Michael Greene, gave with his expert advice, research, and editing.

Thanks also go to Beth, Brian, Keith, and Joel for their support and to my late grandmother, Margaret Greene, and my late aunt Kathleen Vieser for their contributions of family stories.

INTRODUCTION

Unsung Hero is a tribute to all service members who supported our country in whatever capacity throughout our history and today. One of those heroes was my father, Albert V. Greene, who served his country during World War II as a prisoner of war (POW). Dad returned to civilian life while remaining in the Army Reserve. He then reenlisted and served in the Korean War and later served in Vietnam.

If you are among those heroes or know or support them, you will find the stories in this book informative and introspective. I hope this book will inspire you to share your own stories so future generations will not forget and will learn from history.

Unsung Hero serves as a biography and cultural history sharing the life of Albert Vincent Greene through his family story, starting with immigration during the late 1800s from Germany and Ireland to Brooklyn, New York. The narrative continues with Al's recollection of his father's military service during the Great War. This biographical section describes Al's life before World War II, after the war, and through the Cold War, when he served in Korea, Hawaii, the continental United States, Germany during the Berlin Crisis, and Vietnam at the height of the Tet Offensive.

After twenty-five years of military service, Al completed his education and taught the future of America. He put up a good fight against his last battle with Alzheimer's disease, or dementia, and succumbed in 2009. He was laid to rest among other heroes at Arlington National Cemetery.

Unsung Hero also contains my father's memoir of his World War II and POW experiences. Written after many requests, his manuscript reveals what he, like many of the Greatest Generation, did not share about service in World War II. He fought in the Italian Campaign during his service from March 31, 1943, to December 1, 1945. It is the story of a young man from Brooklyn who fought in Italy and was then captured and imprisoned in POW camps. He bravely attempted escape. These experiences came back to haunt him during the last years of his life. How would you have reacted to some of the experiences shared here?

Albert Vincent Greene was definitely an unsung hero. This book is my family's way of singing about one of our country's little-known heroes.

Military abbreviations, jargon, and other colorful language are explained in the glossary. An explanation of military time, poems written by my father while a prisoner, and individual memorials are included at the back of this book.

THE BIOGRAPHY
THE LIFE AND TIMES OF
ALBERT V. GREENE

Captain Greene at Fort Devens, Massachusetts (1957).

My father, Albert Vincent Greene, was born on August 27, 1924, to second-generation Americans of Irish and German descent. His father, Patrick Joseph Greene, a proud veteran of the Great War, came from Irish stock while the parents of his mother, Margaret Loretta Hock, emigrated from Germany. Knowing his roots and background will help us understand the man who became my father, one of the little-known heroes of our country.

The Greenpoint Theatre (1908–1965).

Coming to Greenpoint (1800–1913)

Wherever Al roamed, he considered Greenpoint, Brooklyn, New York, his home. Like many neighborhoods on the East Coast, Greenpoint was full of immigrant families. First the English and the Dutch arrived, sending the local Native Americans packing. Then the Germans came, followed by the Irish in the 1800s.

Greenpoint shared in the economic successes and stresses of Brooklyn and New York. The Industrial Revolution and industrialism had many good and difficult jobs bestowed on the people. Most of Al's male relatives worked on the pier in the thriving shipbuilding industry. Unions were strong, but many workers toiled long hours in unsafe conditions.

Al's grandfather, Francis Xavier Green (1858–1946), emigrated from Ireland to Rhode Island, where he married Annie McCann (1854–1944) in 1886. Both had arrived separately around 1880 through a port in Rhode Island. Later they moved to a small apartment in Greenpoint. Both Francis and Annie were well educated. Francis, a big man who spoke Gaelic and had strong political views, worked as a mason, a stationary engineer, and a hospital watchman.

Francis and Annie had one daughter, Mary (Mae), and four sons, James, John, Francis Jr., and Patrick (Al's father). James died of consumption (tuberculosis) in 1906 at seventeen. In 1918, Francis Jr. and his wife, Serenia, died during the global flu pandemic. Their children, Francis III and Margaret, were raised by their grandparents.

The family name acquired an *e* at the end of it at about this time. The change was never really officially made. Mae had changed it during her early school years in an effort to distinguish their Irish heritage from the many Jewish families in New York with similar names.

Al's mother's side was German. Joseph Anton Hock (1864–1904) had moved from Aschaffenburg in 1882. Known as Anton, he came to the United States to avoid an unpopular conscription into the Prussian army, as did tens of thousands of other Europeans.

Anton met Katerina at Saint Alphonsus Church in Greenpoint, a German parish at the time. Katerina had emigrated from Sendalbach and now worked as a maid for a Dr. Murphy, who lived near Theodore Roosevelt in wealthy Cove Neck on Long Island. She also served at his parties. Anton married Katerina in 1892.

An explosion at the varnish factory where he worked took Anton's life in 1904. This left his young immigrant wife with five children to support. Katerina had carried six children, but only five lived to adulthood. They were John (died as an infant), Margaret (Al's mother), Joseph, William, Francis, and Catherine.

After Anton's death, Katerina was forced to give up her home because she could no longer afford it. She took a job as a maid. She could not care for the children, so they were split up and placed in foundling homes run by the Catholic community. She visited each on the weekends until, one by one, they became old enough to help support the family.

Joseph and William went to the Nazarene Home in Farmingdale. Francis, the baby, stayed in an orphanage in Flushing. Catherine had a heart condition, so she lived in a special home in Far Rockaway. Margaret, the eldest, lived with the nuns at the Convent of Our Lady of Good Counsel in Brooklyn until graduating from eighth grade. Between 1908 (age fourteen) and 1910, she worked at Stern's Department Store, earning three dollars a week. Then she took over her mother's job working as a living-out girl for Dr. Murphy. (A living-out girl lived in the home of her employer, not her own residence.)

The children of Katerina and Joseph Anton Hock: Catherine, Margaret, Joseph, Francis, and William (1904).

On the left: Patrick's friend, Joe Hock.
On the right: Patrick.

The Great War (1914–1919)

The First World War started in Europe in 1914 and lasted until 1918. At the time, this war was called the Great War. America entered the conflict in 1917. More than a hundred of Greenpoint's young men died in that war. Al's father, Patrick, had been studying to be a lawyer, but he quit school to serve in the Army. He enlisted on June 22, 1916.

Patrick's friend from Greenpoint, Joseph Hock, also enlisted in the Army, and the two continued their friendship throughout their service. Patrick served first with Company F of the 47th Infantry Regiment and later transferred to Company E, 53rd Pioneer Infantry. He made corporal on August 20, 1917. Patrick and Joe fought side by side in the trenches of Europe.

Margaret Hock, Joe Hock's sister, traveled to Patrick's post in New York to visit with her brother. But as luck would have it, Joe was not there. This gave Margaret and Patrick the chance to talk awhile. He asked if he could write to her while he was overseas, and she agreed. This wartime long-distance relationship would result in their marriage after the war.

Patrick trained in the United States with the infantry for nearly a year and was shipped "over there" in May 1918, landing at Brest, France. For the first few months in France, his unit trained with British and French units. They also dug trenches and played poker. When combat came, Patrick fought alongside his friend, Joe. Their first action was the successful assault and capture of Sergy.

The American Expeditionary Force (AEF) was new and untested, so the European commanders insisted on placing the AEF command under the French. Soon the Americans got their chance to prove their battle worthiness when their forces were pinched in a geographically inverted V called the Saint Mihiel Salient.

American commanders distinguished themselves from the Europeans in combat. Whereas the European commanders issued orders from their headquarters behind the lines, American commanders like Colonel George Patton and Brigadier General Douglas MacArthur led their men from the front. This way, the American leaders could quickly react to changes on the front. (Patton and MacArthur served both in WWI and WWII.)

The American enlisted men impressed the Europeans with the sheer speed of their advance. For instance, when faced with "impenetrable" barbed wire, the British and French forces would typically rely on artillery or tanks to make a hole for the infantry. American soldiers, however, simply stepped over the wire in the heat of battle, and demonstrated a kinetic force that moved much faster than any other army on the field.

The next campaign, the Meuse-Argonne Offensive, involved a million American soldiers fighting for forty-seven days in the bloodiest campaign of the war. Patrick and Joe were there from September 26 until the end of the war on the eleventh hour of the eleventh day of the eleventh month of 1918. Today we call it Veteran's Day.

During that action, a grenade exploded at the top of a trench near Patrick. Al recalled the story that Joe told him:

> *My father stood up in the trench, and a grenade landed behind him. Shrapnel went everywhere. Patrick was the only one hit. They thought he was dead, and so they bugged out through the trenches without him. After a while, they came back to recover the body. Someone picked Patrick's body up to throw it into a wagon and noticed his finger moving. That saved his life.*

Shrapnel entered Patrick's skull from the back and exited behind his ear, with part of the metal wedged inside his brain. Once he was found and taken to a hospital in France, a nurse named Kathleen stayed with him and helped him through surgery. (Patrick later named his daughter after that nurse.) Surgeons were unable to remove all the shrapnel, so Patrick lost hearing in one ear and suffered severe neuropathy and excruciating headaches the rest of his life.

Sergeant Patrick Greene was discharged with a disability on February 25, 1919. He worked in civilian life as a federal postal employee but always considered himself a soldier. He served on many military boards and veteran organizations. His medals included the Purple Heart, the Victory Medal, the Conspicuous Service Medal, and the New York State War Service Medal. They are on display, along with Albert's, in the military exhibition at the Eisenhower Recreation Center in The Villages, Florida.

Corporal Patrick Greene during the Great War.

Patrick and Margaret Greene (July 1919).

The Patrick Greene Family (1919–1929)

After "the war to end all wars," manufacturing thrived, and Americans had plenty of spending money. During the 1920s, women gained the right to vote. Prohibition banned the manufacture and sale of alcohol. Organized crime delivered booze to illegal bars called speakeasies. Violent gangs in Greenpoint, both Italian and Irish, caused trouble. The Roaring Twenties ushered in great social changes due to both prosperity and violence.

Joe found a job as a trolley conductor in Greenpoint. Patrick went to work as a machinist. Margaret Hock, Joe's sister and Patrick's girlfriend, continued working as a living-out girl for Dr. Murphy until she and Patrick married in July 1919. Since apartments were difficult to find, Patrick continued living with his parents and Margaret stayed with the Murphys, even after she and Patrick married.

Their first child, Kathleen, was named for the nurse Patrick credited with saving his life in France. After Kathleen's birth, the family moved into a farmhouse in Queens Village. Later they moved to a three-flat apartment (three rooms) on Monroe Street in Brooklyn, where James was born. Then they moved to another three-flat on Clifford Place, where Patrick Jr. was born. They moved again, this time to Jewel Avenue, where Albert was born. In his words:

> *We were all very good children. Neither my father nor mother struck us. Mom used what today would be called a time-out. I remember having to stay in my chair or in a corner until the big hand on our clock moved five minutes. Those were the longest five minutes of my young life.*

Both Kathleen and Al would walk to St. Cecelia's School about a mile from their house every morning, then trod back for lunch, went back for the afternoon session, and then walked home after school. "Before I started school, Kathleen took me for a walk after lunch.

When we got to Winthrop Park, she told me to stay on the park bench and wait for her to go home. Then she went to school. Well…" Al shook his head in disbelief. "I stayed right there."

"Yes," Kathleen said. "He was exactly where I left him when I returned."

"What Kathleen didn't know," Al said, "was an old man heard her tell me to stay. The gentleman stayed right there with me. And every time I got up, he made sure I'd stay."

Patrick Sr. worked for the US Postal Service. Al described his father at work:

> *He was the fastest mail separator in that office. He had a machine that he practiced on whenever he was going back to work. He sure was fast. But he was injured in the war and had a metal plate in the back of his head. The headaches were so bad he often could not get out of bed.*

On many days, Al took a nickel for the public phone, called the post office, and said, "Patrick Greene is sick today. He cannot come into work." Patrick was considered a local war hero. On his days off, he practiced sorting mail and became the fastest sorter at his station.

The Greenes lived in a large six-flat or "railroad" apartment on Engert Avenue in Greenpoint. A six-flat meant six rooms went from front to back with one window in front and one in back, like cars lined up on a railroad track. The entire flat had no walls to divide rooms, but rather a long corridor went through them.

Their apartment was also a cold-water flat. There was no heat other than a black potbelly stove. Light came from candles or kerosene lanterns. Margaret washed clothes in a wooden tub using a corrugated washboard and then hung the laundry on a pulley-style clothesline attached to the third-floor window and connected between apartment buildings.

Patrick could drive, but they never owned a car. He had been in an accident once, went to the hospital, and decided he didn't need a car. Public transportation was very good. They also walked a lot.

Margaret played the piano. Patrick played tunes by ear even though he lost most of his hearing in the Great War. Each child had to learn to play and sing one song on the piano. They would stand around the family's player piano and sing in harmony. They all learned to play the Jew's harp and the bazooka. The boys also learned to play the harmonica.

Margaret stayed at home, handling all of the household affairs. The family circumstances always stayed humble. It seemed as if the financial fortunes of the Roaring Twenties had passed them by.

The Great Depression (1929–1939)

The Great Depression affected the entire world. Patrick, however, didn't lose his job at the post office. He always said, "Work for the government; you'll never get laid off."

Although making and selling alcoholic beverages was illegal, drinking them was not. Many of the men in the neighborhood, Patrick included, often dropped by the local speakeasy. He was paid every two weeks, so he'd stop at the corner bar, buy a drink for everyone in the house, and go home. Margaret used whatever money was left over to keep the family fed and clothed. Kathleen explained:

> *Salaries were small. Our aunt Catherine worked for $13.08 per week. My father earned $40.08 at the post office. You could buy soles for shoes and glue them on yourself for only ten cents. My mother mended all our shoes. She also sewed our clothes and took old coats apart to fit them to our sizes.*

> *We had no money, but we were not poor. All our relatives, cousins, aunts, and uncles lived in the same area, so when one person outgrew their clothes or shoes, we'd get their stuff. It was used, but new to us. The boys received their suits, jackets, and coats from relatives. I always had pretty dresses Mama bought for a quarter at the Salvation Army.*

Al told this story:

> *We never went hungry. We pretty much ate the same thing every day. A friend of my brother James used to come over to the house for dinner. He said, "You people sure must like potatoes because that's all you eat." All we had were potatoes. My mother knew*

how to make potatoes more ways than you can shake a stick at. Mama always bought her groceries at Vogel's Grocery. We had no money and had to charge everything. We started that on Jewel Street, and when we moved to Engert Avenue, we still went all the way to Vogel's.

The Greene children, their cousins, and the neighborhood kids played stickball in the streets. (There were few cars.) Young Patrick was a two-and-a-half-sewer man. That meant he could hit the ball and it would go a block and a half, or two and a half sewers, before it came down.

The boys often walked over to swim in Whale Creek, which was part of Newtown Creek, one of the busiest bodies of water in America. Newtown Creek was always full of logs, so they all tried logrolling. Because Newtown Creek was so busy, Patrick placed it off-limits to his sons, so when the boys wanted to go, Kathleen threw their swim suits out the window so their parents wouldn't know.

During the day, the children, James, Patrick, Kathleen, and Albert, attended grade school at St. Cecilia's School. Al said:

We started in first grade and stayed with the same class through grade eight. Mr. Stumpler used to come to the house once a month to collect ten cents from my mother so we could go to St. Cecelia's School. But we couldn't always afford that.

Mr. Strumpler would say, "Well, Mrs. Greene, do you have five cents? A penny?"

"No," she'd say. "It'll just have to wait."

And it did wait.

14

After a short pause, Al continued:

I remember that all the World War One veterans received a bonus. The bonus was one thousand dollars. The next day, Mr. Vogel, the grocer, knocked on the door. The bill we'd racked up was eight hundred dollars. She also paid off Mr. Stumpler, the school guy. Then there was nothing left.

Al stuffed mattresses for a while and delivered dry-cleaning.

I worked after school. Well, for a day or two at each job. When it got too difficult for too little pay, I quit. I wanted to set up a shoeshine business. All the other boys had one and made good money, but when I asked my father, he said, "No son of mine is going to kneel down to anyone."

I really made money selling papers. Daily newspapers sold for two cents, but I had to first buy them in order to sell them. Each paper cost me a penny and a half. So I'd buy a couple dollars' worth and go from bar to bar, selling them for two cents each. I made half a cent on every paper. Saturday was big money. I'd buy the news for three cents and sell it for a nickel.

Plenty of news filled the papers in the 1930s. The government convicted Al Capone, a notorious gangster who once lived in Greenpoint, of tax evasion. Franklin Delano Roosevelt became president in 1933 and launched the New Deal, creating federal programs aimed at putting Americans back to work and helping agriculture. He enacted Social Security and federal jobs programs. A constitutional amendment in 1933 repealed prohibition.

In 1933, Adolf Hitler became chancellor of Germany. Benito Mussolini, the fascist dictator of Italy, invaded Ethiopia. In 1937,

Japan invaded China. Hitler consolidated political power and created a Nazi dictatorship.

During this time, Al's father continued working in the postal service. His mother stayed at home. On September 1, 1939, the German army invaded Poland in a fast-moving *blitzkrieg* attack. The Second World War began in Europe. The British and French fought the Germans, but America stayed out of the war for a couple years. Instead the United States sent war supplies across the ocean to support the French and British. Then the Empire of Japan bombed Pearl Harbor.

Kathleen learned of the attack while at a dance in the basketball gym of the Loughlin Lyceum at St. Cecilia's Church. The news spread wildly, and everyone went home stunned. The family sat around their kitchen table listening to President Roosevelt's speech on the radio:

> *Yesterday, December 7th, 1941—a date which will live in infamy—the United States of America was suddenly and deliberately attacked by naval and air forces of the Empire of Japan...*

The attack on the naval base at Pearl Harbor, Hawaii, then a territory of the United States, killed more than 2,400 Americans, destroyed the battleship USS *Arizona*, capsized the USS *Oklahoma*, and sank or damaged 21 other ships and 310 aircraft.

The United States was at war.

The Greenes Go to War (1939–1945)

Everybody had a part to play during the war. With many men overseas, women worked in the factories. With much military demand for every kind of thing, civilian purchase of many items was rationed, especially gasoline, meat, and rubber tires. The government asked people to invest in war bonds and grow their own food. Even in the cities, families tended to their own victory gardens.

At the beginning of the war, Al was too young to serve. Patrick Sr. worked at the post office when he was able. He also spent much of his time serving on various patriotic and veteran boards. He was a member of Veterans of Foreign Wars, T. R. Nalty Post; commander of the VFW George Black Post; welfare officer of Kings County VFW; and post adjutant of the Greenpoint Catholic War Veterans.

When Jimmy, Albert, and their brother Patrick went into the service, their mother Margaret said she was not going to stay home and worry, so she got a job at Shivers Bookbindery on the north side of Greenpoint. She also worked for the Red Cross. She and Kathleen knit socks and head covers for the soldiers.

Kathleen attended school and worked at Gertz Department Store, where she met a young man named Cyril Vieser who joined the US Army Air Corps and served in Baffinland. Cyril and Kathleen married on November 12, 1944. Their daughter Maureen was born in 1946.

James, the first of the brothers to enlist, was not yet eighteen, so Kathleen signed his father's name to his enlistment form. Jimmy, as he was known, enlisted June 5, 1939, and joined the 165th Infantry Regiment, which was comprised entirely of men from New York City.

Stationed in Hawaii, he served in the Pacific Theater. His unit fought victoriously against the Japanese in the Makin Atoll, Saipan, and Okinawa. His duty ended on August 27, 1945. He attained the rank of staff sergeant. First to enlist, Jimmy was the last of the brothers to return. In 1947, Jimmy married Florence Bombino in 1947. They had two children, Patricia and James. Jimmy died in 1959.

Patrick Jr. enlisted in the Army on Al's birthday, August 27, 1942. He attended parachute training at Fort Benning and then was sent to a replacement depot at Camp Reynolds, Pennsylvania, where he processed thousands of soldiers for duty overseas. He transferred overseas to Europe in 1944.

After the war, Patrick married a girl he had met at Camp Reynolds, Mary Cowan. Then he served the people of Sharpsville, Pennsylvania, as a fireman and police officer. He eventually retired as the police chief. Patrick and Mary had three boys and a girl: Raymond, Patrick III, Tommy, and Mary Anne.

Not liking school, Al quit in 1942. He was seventeen years old. His father had some influence on the local draft board. Not wanting Margaret to risk losing all her sons during the war, Patrick persuaded the board to keep Al off the draft rolls.

At the same time, he persuaded his youngest son that he must never volunteer. "If they need you, they will call."

So Al lived at home and worked at various jobs while waiting for a draft notice that did not come. Once Al discovered how his father was keeping him out of the war, he confronted him. "I didn't volunteer, and now I find that you're keeping me here! I want to go!"

"There was such a fight," Kathleen said. "But Pop went down to the draft board and had Al's name reinstated."

Al became the only Greene boy drafted. He reported for duty on March 31, 1943.

Top: Albert, Kathleen, Patrick Sr., Margaret, and Patrick Jr. (1943).
Bottom: Cyril Vieser married Al's sister, Kathleen.

Jimmy and Albert during World War II.

Margaret Hock Greene (1943).

WORLD WAR II EXPERIENCES OF ALBERT V. GREENE THE MEMOIR

Private Greene at induction (1943).

Induction

I am a private first class (PFC) in the Army of the United States (AUS). "First class" just means I got four bucks a month more than a private. I was in the Army for two and a half years. I traveled considerably, saw quite a few things, and met up with many different people, some good and others bad. In this story, I'll try to omit the bad ones.

My story starts on 31 March 1943, the day I reported for induction into the AUS for the duration—until the war is over plus six months. I left with two hundred other guys and a brass band. It seemed that all of Greenpoint, the town I come from in Brooklyn, New York, turned out.

As I was leaving my home on Flatbush Avenue, I told my mom that I didn't want to see any tears. I had two brothers in the Army, and I was the last boy in the family to go and the only one in my family to be drafted. I was eighteen years old.

My father's farewell advice was, "Remember that one minute of pleasure can cause a lifetime of sorrow."

I was accepted for "limited service" and taken to Camp Upton, Long Island. I was there for only three days getting processed. A group of us was taken to the railroad station and told that we were on our way to an army camp for training. Was I surprised when the train stopped at Flatbush Avenue!

We were loaded onto trucks and taken to Fort Hamilton in Brooklyn, New York, just one and a half hour travel time from my house. That was quite a break for me. I didn't realize it at the time, but I certainly do now. This took place on Saturday, 3 April 1943. I got a weekend pass starting that same day. I certainly looked smart in my new uniform. At least I thought I did.

I was with the medics in the Fort Hamilton station hospital for the following six weeks until I got into a little trouble. I had an argument with a corporal and then with a second lieutenant. I had my choice of either a court-martial or doing KP permanently. I took the latter because my dad was a soldier at heart, and I knew he wouldn't want me to be court-martialed. I was transferred to the Staten Island terminal to do permanent KP.

There was no extra pay for this, as it was just my regular-duty assignment. I did my work with plenty of griping, and I do mean plenty. I had hoped from the start of my army career that I would go into the infantry just like my brothers. I went to see the medics about getting reclassified to 1A. (Local draft boards classified all men for eligibility to serve. Men classified 1A were eligible for unlimited military service.)

I really wanted the infantry. After a while, I was made a 1A man. I put in for a transfer to the infantry, but all I got was the job of helping to operate a gas station in Staten Island, New York. After seven months of KP, I started on a three-month gas-and-oil man job. Again I put in for a transfer to the infantry. Once again I was transferred, but not into the infantry. I was sent to work as a clerk in the army post office in New York City.

I was now only thirty minutes from home, but I was still not satisfied. I sweated out three months in Company A, Postal Battalion, before I wrote to the adjutant general in Washington, DC. I was determined to get into the infantry. If it took a general's word to get me into the infantry, I was going to get that word.

I finally got that long-awaited transfer to the infantry. I went down to Camp Rucker, Alabama, finished my basic training, and then went home on furlough. Upon returning from leave, I went to Fort Meade, Maryland, to wait for shipping orders to go to a point of embarkation.

I stayed at Fort Meade about a week before I went to Camp Peter Stuyvesant, Massachusetts. There, I got an overnight pass and went home. I saw my folks for about an hour. It was well worth the train fare. The day after coming back from that pass 22 September, I embarked for overseas.

Landing ships used in World War II.

England and France

I landed in England 10 October 1944, and found it just as everyone had described it—foggy, rainy, and mud-covered. It was not the ideal spot to be in. While I was in Warminster, England, I got a pass to visit Trowbridge, a nice little town with nothing more to do for entertainment than go to a show. The name of the picture was *Flight to Freedom*. It was quite an old film.

When I returned from the pass, we were put on alert. We were destined to go to France. We were paid in francs and had all our American and British currency converted into French money. I was supposed to get a pass to visit my sister's boyfriend's grandmother in Kent when we went to Southampton. That was quite the mudhole. It was even worse than Warminster. You'll read quite a bit about mud before you finish this. Mud played a prominent part in the war.

We boarded a Liberty ship and set underway to cross the English Channel. It was quite an experience. When we were in sight of France, we were transferred onto landing ships (LSTs) that were capable of ferrying tanks. We landed on Omaha Beach in Normandy. It was a sight that I won't forget for as long as I live. To this day, I still can't figure out how the dogfaces ever succeeded in making the landing there during the invasion on D-day.

For the first hundred yards, it was just a sandy beach with no cover or concealment. For the next two hundred yards, the boys had to climb a steep cliff. A good number of our boys must have been hit on that particular beach.

We walked through the mud for about two hours before we were told to pitch our tents. Yes, right in the middle of a big muddy field, we pitched our tents. This was nothing, I assure you. At least we didn't have to dig foxholes…yet.

We were in France for just about a week when we got orders to go to Cherbourg Airport. We boarded trucks and went to the airport. Quite a few C-47 troop-carrying airplanes were on the field. I set up my shelter half under the wing of one of the planes, so when it started to rain, I was okay. You should have seen some of my buddies who slept out in the open without a tent. When they woke up, they were soaked. I still don't know how they slept through it. When morning came, we boarded the planes and took off. It was my first airplane hop, so I was pretty excited.

Italy

After eight hours, we finally landed. Where? In Italy. We all started to sing, "Where do we go from here, boys? Where do we go from here?"

A Louie (lieutenant), who was a pretty nice Joe (regular guy), answered that question promptly, "Pisa."

We went through Pisa in GI trucks and passed right by the Leaning Tower. I was seeing things of interest at the Army's expense.

The rest of the town was pretty well shot up. It wasn't a lovely sight to see people begging for food or cigarettes. Children were pathetically looking for chewing gum or candy.

After about an hour or so on the trucks, we stopped at the reppie deppie (replacement depot). We got off the trucks, formed a column of ducks (twos), and marched off to the firing range. We zeroed in our rifles until it was too dark to see the targets, and then we marched back. We were housed in ten-man tents with cots. (That was a luxury.) We drew so much clothing and protective clothing that we didn't know what to do with it all. We just put it into our B-bags and forgot about it for the time being. After all, we didn't have to worry about protection from gas. We let the frontline boys worry about that. Well, in a few days, I was one of those frontline boys.

The post exchange (PX) came around, and each of us was allowed ten bottles of beer. I didn't care too much for the stuff at the time, so I took it to town and swapped it to the Ities (Italians) for *vino* (wine). I got stinkin' drunk that night with *vino rosa* (red wine). It's really belly rot. I got back to the reppie deppie in an unsoberly condition, to say the least.

In a few days, we boarded trucks and started for the front. We traveled all night in those overstuffed GI wagons and got pretty stiff. We pulled up on the side of the road and piled out.

We could hear the rumble of the big guns when we de-trucked. We left our B-bags on the truck and made up packs to carry with us.

I had three blankets, one shelter half, one raincoat, and an overcoat. It was pretty heavy.

We marched all day long, throwing away our clothing little by little. We were told that we were replacements for the 88th Infantry Division (Blue Devils). That made no difference to me because I had never heard of them. I forgot that there had been a war on in Italy since D-day in France. I was sent to Company K of the 349th Regiment. I didn't want to go to any Company K, 349th Regiment, 88th Infantry Division anymore. I just wanted to go home. I'd had enough of the mud and slop already.

However, I went to the Blue Devil division. When we were segregated and finally settled, I heard a soft but rough voice ask, "Hey, you guys, what outfit are you in?"

I told him, and he said to follow him. So I did.

I was told to buddy up with one of the old-timers in the outfit. I tried to, but when I told them that my name was Greene, none of them would have me. I was a green soldier as far as combat was concerned.

A voice finally popped up and asked me how many blankets I had, so I told him two. I had thrown away one on the road. He said he didn't care if I were green in name or otherwise. He just wanted my blanket. So I buddied up with him. His name doesn't matter as he is no longer with the outfit. As a matter of fact, he is no longer. His foxhole wasn't deep enough, I guess.

Private Greene was the grenadier of his squad, firing rifle grenades at German soldiers during the Italian Campaign. Here is a soldier demonstrating launching a grenade from an M1 Garand rifle, the most commonly used American rifle during World War II.

First Combat

Morning came around very quickly, and I found myself on the front line after a short walk of a mile or so. The outfit was still pushing back the Jerries. The platoon sergeant, PFC Walkerwitz, or something like that, got orders to take seven men and knock out a Jerry machine gun. I was selected as one of the men.

From that day on, I was first scout. All told, we knocked out eight machine guns and an artillery observation post without firing a shot. The Germans saw us coming and just came out with their hands up. They got tired of fighting for a lost cause.

That was my first day of combat. I figured that it would be a cinch. All a guy had to do was show himself, and out came seventy-nine Jerries with their hands up. I found out later just how different it really was. By the way, my friend Johnny got the Silver Star for that deal.

We were pretty busy for the next few weeks, dodging shells and the whiz of bullets. Not the bullets so much as the shells. If you've ever heard a screaming meemie or an 88, you've been in the war and scared too.

As you know, Italy is a pretty cold place around November. That was when I went back to Montecatini with a slight case of trench foot. (Prolonged exposure to cold and wet conditions can lead to amputation.)

I was back for one day when my outfit moved in and took over the town for a rest. For the eight days I spent in the hospital, I wrote quite a few letters. I told the folks that I was in the hospital with a fever and a slight cold, which was true, but I didn't tell them about the trench foot.

I got out of the hospital, only to find that my outfit was ready to move up to the front again. I was very disgusted. I wanted to go to town just like the rest of them, but no dice. We left the next morning.

We had to walk for six miles up and down and around mountains on a mule trail, hardly wide enough for a man, much less a mule. By this time, I had learned not to carry so much equipment with me. However, I did carry my shelter half, raincoat, overcoat, and half-blanket. After reaching the position, we were told that it was going to be static one. We were going to stay for quite a while, and I only had a half blanket.

I manned a foxhole with a buddy of mine, Eugene Guy, who came all the way from the States with me. He was a very quiet sort of fellow and very nervous. He was a good man to have in a foxhole. He never went to sleep on you.

We used to talk about home a lot. He was my confidential buddy. By that, I mean I used to talk about my home affairs and such, and he told me his. He used to tell me about his different girlfriends and bring out pictures and so on. I would have too, only my wallet was picked with all my pictures while I was en route to England.

The first night up was a quiet one. Not a shot or shell fired by the enemy. Our boys on the 60s sent a few shells over, and our 50s rattled a few times, but that was all. We didn't have to worry too much about being in a foxhole in the daytime as we were quartered in a building from which we had good observation.

We cooked our 10-in-1 rations on a small Coleman stove and ate out of canteen cups. We never carried mess kits, as they were useless.

One fellow always carried one, so we could use it for a frying pan. That was Eugene Guy. He carried anything from breakfast cereal to a can of meat and beans. He was quite a character, but a swell guy.

Evening rolled around quickly, and the boys had to man the foxholes again. I was scheduled to go on contact patrols to the British at 1900 and 0200. It was beginning to get more exciting to me, but I still wanted to go home.

At 1900, I started out with the communications sergeant for the contact patrol. I kept a lookout for the Jerries while he checked telephone wires to the British position. There was a large gap between our lines that had to be patrolled at night to make sure the Jerries didn't make any positions there.

We walked on the side of a mountain just about halfway to the position, and we spotted some five or six German-type foxholes. We looked at each other as if to say, "What do we do now?" Neither of us asked the question though.

I grabbed a handful of mud and rounded it out in the shape of a ball. I took a few steps and stopped, made the motion of pulling the pin on a hand grenade, and threw the mud in the direction of the holes. If there were Germans there, they would have opened up. If there were no one there, the mud would just drop soundlessly, and we'd walk on by with no one the wiser. Well, there were no Jerries there, thank God, so we walked on by.

Upon reaching the British position, we sat down for a break. We were pretty tired. About eight Limeys came out with Tommy guns, and we talked for about five minutes. They asked us to bring along some cigarettes and cheese on the next patrol. They'd swap us some sardines and tea for it. We made a good bargain. They took us to the officer in charge, an Irishman. Again we talked for a while, had a cigarette, and called our outfit on the phone. We told them that we were on our way back. We went back using the same precautions as though it was our first time over that terrain.

We got back to the outfit and were told there was to be a combat patrol. I didn't have to go. I went to sleep under my half-blanket and woke up at 0145 with the aid of someone shaking me. I still had a patrol to go on.

I rounded up about a case of K-ration cheeses and quite a few packs of cigarettes and started out. When we got to the Tommies, they gave us the sardines and the tea so we took off for Company K, 2nd Platoon. When we got back, the boys were just coming in from the combat patrol. They had been out with quite a bit of luck. Only one man, the rifle grenadier, was hurt. The Jerries didn't hit him though. He fired his rifle grenade too close to his face, and some of the gas from the exploded round got into his eyes so he could hardly see. He was sent back to the hospital for treatment. The eyes are a very vulnerable spot.

The next day went along as usual, except the boys were still jumpy from the night before. When evening came, I was to have a little more time to sleep. The British were to make the 1900 patrol, and I was to make the 0200 patrol. I went to sleep while the other fellows manned the foxholes.

Around midnight, all hell broke loose outside. I jumped and grabbed my rifle and went to the rear of the building. There I stayed. I was scared, and I don't mean maybe. There was only one way out of the house, through the front door.

Jerry blew that door open three times, but after each time, someone ran up and closed it. If we hadn't closed the door, a rifle grenade was bound to come whizzing in. No one fired back at Jerry, so he took off after twenty minutes of raising hell. When they left, we had five casualties. Jerry did a good job: one man dead and four wounded.

I had to man one of the foxholes then, as we were short of men. I didn't go on that second hop. I was in the front hole with Harry Green, who had come from England with me. He told me that his buddy Guiderelli was one of the wounded. He asked to buddy with me, so the two Green(e) boys were buddies. I was more green than he was, as he saw action with the Canadian army at the evacuation of Dieppe.

The remainder of the night went slowly as we were very jumpy, cold, and scared. About 0300, I heard a sound just below our hole. I told Harry what I had heard, but he said that was my imagination. We conversed for about fifteen minutes before I threw out a grenade. When it exploded and I heard nothing more, I was set at ease. So was Harry.

Morning came, but the fog had rolled in to stay, so we also had to stay in our holes. It started to drizzle and got very cold. Harry took off his shoes and wrapped up his feet in a blanket. I was too scared to take off my shoes. My feet were freezing, and I could only wiggle my toes. Sometimes I couldn't even do that.

Everything went smooth—but cold—for the next few days until Thanksgiving Day. We had C-rations that could never do, so we organized a patrol to see what kind of game we could work up. We wound up with about forty-five pounds of rabbit and six chickens. That wasn't a bad meal, although I thought I'd get sick after watching the fellows kill and skin them. It was something for a city boy like myself not to see. We had a good meal all right, but we had a tough time digesting it because there was to be another combat patrol that night.

We took off with Harry and me as scouts. Our mission was to take a prisoner, a live one. We passed our roadblock and headed toward Jerryland. We walked for about a quarter mile before we ran into their roadblock.

Bullets flew and grenades hit their marks. Their machine gun was knocked out so we ran in, grabbed a wounded Jerry, and dragged him back. While we were on our way back, one of our boys stepped on a shoe mine. He also had to be dragged back.

We turned over our prisoner and our wounded man to the medics for treatment. I didn't hear from either thereafter. That's the biggest problem in the infantry. As soon as you make friends, you lose 'em some way or another.

We were relieved the following evening and had that six-mile walk through the mud again. The almost knee-high mud was like gooey cement. When you put your foot into it, you have a tough time pulling it out again. The mud would pack on the bottom of your shoes, and it would make you so much the heavier. Men would fall down fifteen or twenty times. I was one of the men who fell continuously. My rifle was so full of mud that it wouldn't fire even if I wanted it to. They should have called us "mud faces" instead of dogfaces.

Shrapnel Valley

We marched off the muddy mountain trail to a valley that we soon called "Shrapnel Valley." We were put into ten-man tents again, but this time we had no cots, just the hard ground, which was soon turned into mud after continuous walking on it. Several large field artillery pieces there sounded off only when we wanted to get some sleep.

After a few days rolled by, with a little rain now and then, Jerry rolled up a self-propelled gun (SP) and dropped in about eight rounds. He only got a few men, and they were not in my platoon.

We were paid, and the PX came. We stocked up on chewing gum, candy, and beer, but we had to take off for the front the next day. Some of the boys and I decided that we didn't want the Jerries to get our money in the event that something happened so we decided to start a crap game. We rolled out a blanket and shot craps against a wooden box. Well, I went away broke, as usual.

Morning came quickly. It always does when you are waiting to go to the front. So I put a few bottles of beer in my pack along with my clothes, and we took off. We had hand grenades hanging from our belts and pack straps. I also had a few in my pockets. I was a firm believer in the power of a hand grenade.

When we started up the same mud trail, we all thought that we were going back to the same position, but no dice. We walked a little farther to the left flank of the old position. We didn't like this at all, as we had no house to stay in during the daytime. However, we had caves to stay in on the reverse slope of a hill, facing away from the enemy. We could walk around in the daytime. I didn't have to go on any contact patrols because we had visual contact with other platoons that were on our flanks.

No sooner did we get to the positions when I was told that Harry and I were to man observation post number two (OP #2), which was halfway down the side of a mountain. Visibility was pretty poor so we had to rely more or less on our hearing. Maybe that's where I got my big ears. We had nothing more than a few shells come in that night, but still that was a few shells too many. We went back to our positions just before it got too bright.

We cooked up our C-rations and ate breakfast: a can of frankfurters and beans and some hard crackers and Nescafé. I settled down in my shelter and dozed off to sleep.

I didn't wake up until it was just about time to go back to the OP. I was handed my first bit of mail just then, and my morale really climbed the ladder. After reading a few letters from home and my girlfriend, I was ready to go out and lick the whole German army. I knew I couldn't do it, but that's just the way I felt. Mail from home really pepped up a fellow. Anyone can tell you that.

Harry and I manned OP #1 that night, and what a miserable night that was. Observation was limited to about ten yards, and we could only hear the rain bouncing off our steel helmets. Harry and I took turns sleeping that night. None of us slept any, but we had a chance to rest our eyes. It gets so bad at times that all you can see is a big blank space in front of you. The ground seems to swallow up the road and the little undergrowth nearby. That's when you tell your buddy to take over.

It was getting a little light out, so I went to find out what time it was. I got up on the road and walked toward the next foxhole when a voice rang out with a "Halt." I halted, but I'll be damned if I could remember the password.

I bent over to see who was in the hole when a grenade lit about ten feet from me. I dove into the ditch on the side of the road and yelled to the guy that I was "Greene" and I wanted to find out the time. He said I sure as hell was green to seek cover when I was challenged. I explained the situation to him, so he apologized for heaving the grenade at me and told me the time.

It was time to get back to the caves for the day, so we took off. From that time on, every time I saw that same ugly guy, I sang, "Don't throw grenades at me" to the tune of "People Will Say We're In Love."

After chow that morning, Jerry started to drop in a few mortar shells on us, so everyone made a scramble for the nearest cave for protection. The first shell that came in got one of our boys in the thigh. It was the second time he got hit. When nightfall came, he had to walk all the way to the rear over the muddy mule trail with a piece of shrapnel in his leg. He was a game guy and a swell one.

Our platoon aid man, Chubby Spenser from Oklahoma, fixed him up pretty well. Chubby knew his business. He started out with the division in Camp Gruber, Oklahoma. I saw him work on the wounded men when the shells and bullets were flying all over the place. He was wounded twice as well. He holds the Bronze Star for his good work.

We had a combat patrol scheduled for that night, so everyone was nervous. Everyone—and I mean everyone—dreaded going out to meet the enemy. Our platoon leader, Lieutenant Lynch, was a regular fellow, but he was GI when it came to business. His motto was, "Whoever goes out on patrol comes back, regardless of the condition he comes back in." He said that not one of his men would ever be left alone in No Man's Land, and we respected him for that.

Harry Green and I were scouts again that night. We left shortly after 2200 and ran into Jerry less than twenty-five minutes later. Jerry had positions dug in outside a house, just like we did in our last position. All hell broke loose when Jerry spotted us. Burp guns and Tommy guns neutralized each other's fire. So did their machine guns and our BARs. There was nothing but rifles to cope with.

Lieutenant Lynch gave orders to go to the left flank of the house, heave a few grenades at the Jerries in the slit trenches, and try to take a prisoner. We knocked out the positions outside the house, but some live Jerries were still inside, so we fired a few rifle grenades into the building and then let go with a smoke grenade. We dashed into the building, grabbed off two Jerries, and ran like hell back to our positions. We didn't lose a man, and no one got scratched.

We did a swell job, even if I have to say so myself. When we got back, we manned the foxholes again and started to worry about the next patrol. That's one thing about combat men. They worry and get awfully scared just before and after a patrol. While the fight is in progress, his fears and worries leave him, at least most of the time.

A few more days rolled by with just a few shells coming and going, but nothing of importance happened. When a man is in a foxhole night after night, with no one to talk to about his personal affairs, he does a lot of thinking. He thinks of his folks back home and his girl, mostly about his girl. That keeps him going when he's tired, dirty, and cold. She is part of him, the part that keeps him going.

The time had come for my outfit to be pulled off the line for a while. I was in the OP at the bottom of the hill when the order came down. A fellow from a newly arrived outfit came down to relieve me. My overcoat was so full of mud that it seemed to weigh a ton, so I left it behind. We straggled along the mule trail until we got to the bottom of the mountain. A fleet of trucks was waiting to take us to Garigliano. We weren't all on the trucks when Jerry sent a barrage of SPs into the valley. There were quite a few casualties, thus the name Shrapnel Valley.

We got to Garigliano, a small town about twenty-one kilometers from Florence, early the next morning. We put up platoon tents and got some straw from a nearby straw stack on a farm. The Ities were very nice to us, so we hired three of the men to do our KP for us. We paid them in food by feeding their family. Two of the girls from the family did our laundry. We paid them in money, candy, and soap for their trouble.

I was fortunate enough to get to Florence a few times on one-day passes. We didn't have any clean clothes when I got my first pass to Florence. I was walking through the streets with Harry when a woman in the Women's Army Corps (WAC) came up and asked, "Don't you fellows ever wash and change clothes?"

Harry wanted to take a crack at her, but I changed his mind. He just said, if he were a rear echelon man, he might have had the time. The WAC blushed and rapidly walked away.

I was in Florence on Christmas Day and had a swell turkey dinner with all the trimmings. We even had wine. All this just cost us ten cents in a GI restaurant. Every time I went to Florence, I wanted to stay there, but I never did. It started to snow in Florence, and we knew it was going to be rough going. Besides the mud, we now had to contend with snow and ice.

The day after Christmas, we got our PX and boarded trucks for the front. This was to be a different position, we were told. It was. And believe me, it was a vacation. We didn't have replacements in, so I felt good. That made me an old hand at the combat game. I was able to give advice now as well as ask for it. It's no shame to ask for advice.

My father always told me, "A fool's advice is better than none."

Private Greene in Florence, Italy (Christmas 1944).

Getting a Jerry

Orders came from headquarters that K Company was to get a Jerry. I guess they wanted information in a bad way, as we were never hounded like that before.

Men were selected from all the platoons to go on that patrol. I was one of the selected. Again I was to be a scout. We started out at 0200 to get that Jerry when he was not expecting us. But he was, and we got chased right back. Believe me, we sweated. We sweated from the time we got back to our positions until orders came from HQ that we wouldn't have to go back the following night. When that news came, we all let go with a sigh of relief.

Jerry sent in quite a few shells that day, and he really scared the hell out of us. He took away part of our building with a mortar. The house shook, and we shook with it. We were so shaken up that in time it became a joke among us. We were more scared than most of the replacements. Some of them didn't know enough to be scared.

We didn't have to go to Jerry's house that night because he came to ours. One stayed for lunch. I just turned right when one of our OPs spotted the Jerries fording the river about 150 yards from our house.

The lieutenant set a quick trap. Five of us dashed out undercover to the extreme right flank of the house. Jerry was coming from the rear. The remainder of the platoon got into a frontal position to lay down a base of fire. Jerry got to within thirty-five yards before the entire platoon opened up on them, all except the five of us that went around to the flank. We just waited.

Jerry sent some men around the flank to try to knock out our base of fire. They crawled right into our trap. One got away, but we counted six dead Jerries and sent them back to be buried. We also got three live German prisoners.

We got what we wanted, so we sat back for a few days, gloating over our efficiency.

Manzuno

After we were sufficiently rested, we had to go on a recon patrol to see if the Jerries were still occupying that house. We set out just as soon as it got dark enough. We walked up to within 150 yards of the house when we stopped and took cover. A small group set out for the house and returned fifteen minutes later. They told us that the house was empty.

We reconnoitered around the house again to make sure. We looked for booby traps on the door and windows and found none. Lieutenant Lynch told me to fire a rifle grenade into the door without pulling the pin on the grenade. I fired, and the door flew open. We entered the house and found it to be empty except for some broken-down furniture.

We went back to our positions and reported our findings. There was a rumor that someone was to put in long hours in the cold and snowy foxholes. We were getting food and mail brought up to us on mules. Both items were necessary to keep the infantry in good condition.

We sweated out shells for ten days and were put in reserve. I couldn't figure it out. We were getting too much of a break. Everyone figured that we were being saved for the big push into the Po Valley. We took over the foxholes in the reserve position and made livable quarters out of them.

I bunked with Eugene Guy in that position. He really did the entire interior decorating of our two-man foxhole. He had thick beams over the top and then a shelter half. Piled on top of that, he had a foot of dirt and rocks. The snow did the job of camouflage.

I was sent to the town of Lozano to take instructions on the .50-caliber machine gun. I thought that would be a break for me. I figured I would get out of being a scout and man the .50-caliber for the duration of our static position. But no, they just wanted to make sure that someone knew the .50-caliber just in case the regular man got hit, which he rarely did.

After a few days of living comfortably and receiving mail from home regularly, the Jerries started to send over airbursts. The fellows who didn't have protection from the air soon put boulders and rocks on top of their foxholes. It started to get awfully warm; therefore, the snow started to melt. In less than an hour's time, my foxhole was so full of water that I could have used it for a bathtub. I would have too, only the weather wasn't permitting.

Upon seeing that we could no longer live in foxholes with the usual weather changes, we were sent to board in a few buildings.

I did pretty well. I had a heat generator in my building in the form of a cow. She smelled awful, but the heat she put out was well worth it. We were no longer under observation by the enemy so we could walk around without having to worry about Jerry spotting us. I went to mass that day with Guy. We were supposed to go with another fellow, but he was on detail. While we were in church, Jerry sent a few 88s in on the boys and killed the fellow who was supposed to go with Guy and me.

We left for the front line that night. It was a long walk, longer than usual. We slipped and fell all over the place, only to get back up and go on. The Blue Devils were a determined lot. Nothing could stop them.

We marched into the town of Manzuno and took up positions in the buildings. My platoon drew a lucky straw so we got the house that used to be a hotel. There was a mattress on a spring bed for every man in the platoon. We talked to some of the fellows who were just leaving the position, and they said the place was jumping with action. We thought nothing of it, as that was what they all say. We found it to be a fact the next evening.

We started out on a recon patrol just after darkness. We went about a half mile into No Man's Land, lay down in the snow, and listened. After laying there for an hour or so, the platoon leader took Harry, two other GIs, and me to go on farther. We wanted to find out just where the Jerries were located. We did that. We spotted a Jerry walking into a house, so we took off. We got back shortly after 2300. We didn't have to man foxholes, but we did have to sit in the window and stand outside the building.

The following day, we were told that we were going on a combat patrol to the house we spotted to get that Jerry and bring him back. We couldn't eat a thing that day. Everyone would jump at the slightest noise. We were scared. It was not unusual to be frightened. As a matter of fact, it was unusual not to be.

We started out after nightfall to get that Jerry. We stopped at our roadblock and told them not to fire at us on our way back. We also told them to count the men as we went by. We told him that there would be an extra one when we came back. The boys at the roadblock wished us luck and sent us on our way with some reassuring remark. We got up to within fifty yards of our objective when we were fired upon. We formed a skirmish line along the road and let them have all we could give them.

It wasn't enough. We were driven back. We found it impossible to maneuver around in the white snow without being spotted. We cursed the white snow and wished to hell that it could turn brown. We didn't bring back any prisoner, and we didn't feel bad about it. We were glad that we all got back safely ourselves, much less bring a German prisoner with us. We were all very nervous that night, and we talked among ourselves about what happened.

There was a rumor that someone was going to get a six-day pass to Rome. Everyone prayed that it would have been himself. I must have prayed the hardest because I got it.

When my pass was just about up, I ran into an old buddy of mine that came from the States with me. He told me about a close friend of mine who was reported as missing in action just a few days previous to our meeting. I had to catch the train back to Montecatini so I left my buddy in a hurry.

At the railroad station, I bought a book at the GI canteen and boarded the train. When I finished the book, I was almost in Montecatini. The time on the train went quickly. Trucks were waiting to take us back to our outfits but were not ready to leave, so I bought another book. I was so deeply engrossed in my reading that all the trucks had departed without my knowledge.

There was only one thing left for me to do, hitchhike to the front line. I got a lift from a jeep driver to Florence and ate dinner in one of its fabulous restaurants. After cleaning up, I caught a truck that was going to Lozano.

Upon reaching Lozano, I asked if my outfit were still in its same position, and the reply was positive. I got a lift to the outskirts of Manzuno and walked to company HQ. There I met Harry Green, who was also coming back from pass. He had four days in Montecatini.

We went to our platoon command post, and Harry was told that he was to go home on rotation. He was to be transferred to company HQ for safekeeping. The commanding officer (CO) didn't want anything to happen to him, especially now that he was slated to go home soon. Harry resented being taken out of action and told the CO that he wanted to stay with the company until he rotated.

He definitely wanted at least one more fight before he went home. Harry is a brave man and a swell guy. He always talked about Barney Bradley's Bar. Someday I'll find that place, and Harry will be in there drinking a toast to the 88th Division Blue Devils.

Final Patrol

Things started to happen quickly when I got back, one patrol after another. The second night after my return, we went on a recon patrol but found nothing. The Jerries had evidently moved back. We were destined to find out. The following night was to be a combat patrol with the mission of breaking through their OP to find out what was at position K12.

We lined up on the road in front of the building we were occupying and checked each other out for the final preparation. I carried a basic load of ammunition, six rifle grenades and four hand grenades, including two smoke grenades.

We started out, twenty-eight of us, at about 2030 on 22 February with Harry Green and me as scouts and got as far as Cavalla, which consisted of just a few houses. The platoon leader, Lieutenant Lynch, sent a few men on ahead to check out the building while the rest of us covered them. The buildings were empty, so we continued on down the road to check out K12.

It was really weird. The only thing I could hear was the broken fastener on one of my overshoes that kept making clinking sounds with each step I took. The road down from Cavalla was hard surfaced with a steep chalk line escarpment on the right side until we came to what used to be a town, but all the houses had been leveled by artillery fire.

It was very strange seeing cement steps leading from the road up four steps to where a house used to be. On the left side of the road was an open field that had "Achtung Minen" (Caution Mines) signs posted.

We moved single file past the steps that led to where a couple of houses once stood. Harry was about five yards behind me, followed by our squad leader, Staff Sergeant Evans Murray, and Lieutenant Lynch. The rest of the patrol followed him.

All of a sudden, all hell broke loose. Machine guns, grenades, rapid rifle fire, and flares were blasting away right in front of us. I dove into one of the step areas, fired off the rifle grenade that I had on my grenade launcher, and immediately loaded another. I almost forgot to use a crimped cartridge in the excitement. That would have been the end of me for sure.

Kraut machine gun bullets were bouncing off the concrete in front of the steps, but fortunately I had complete cover from the front, the right side, and the rear. The only way I could have gotten hit was from my left or if I stuck my neck back out on the roadside.

After firing all my rifle grenades and tossing all my hand grenades, I threw a smoke grenade, but unfortunately that only invited more direct fire to my position. I then put my rifle on top of the steps area without looking over the top for obvious reasons, and I fired off clip after clip of ammunition just about as fast as I could. It was just instinctive to return fire whenever you were fired upon. That was taught in basic training, and it was something that came naturally. I had no idea of what I was shooting at, other than the fact that there was no one in front of me except the Krauts.

A potato masher went off right in front of me with such a loud noise that I thought it blew my head off. I wasn't hit, but I couldn't hear a thing except for a loud ringing in my ears for what seemed like an eternity. I kept on firing, clip after clip, until I finally ran out of ammunition.

Everything got very quiet. The Krauts kept sending up one flare after another, keeping the area lit up like broad daylight. When one burned out, they would open up on my position with bullets bouncing all around the roadside, keeping me pinned in the "safe" stairway until they got off another flare.

I noticed early on that there didn't seem to be much in the way of noise coming from behind me, and then I got really scared. I realized that everyone must have been able to get back, or they would certainly have been firing up a storm. There wasn't a sound other than flares going off.

It got as quiet as a church, so I said a few prayers and made all kinds of promises if I could only get out of this situation safely. At least a half hour went by with nothing but flares going off until finally I heard the hobnailed footsteps approaching my position.

Having no ammunition left, I decided I was not about to fix my bayonet and charge the whole German army in front of me, so I dropped my rifle and stepped out onto the road with my hands over my head.

Shaking with Patriotism

I was shaking with patriotism and just stood there while those hobnailed boots ran back to their positions about ten or fifteen yards in front of me. Another flare replaced the one going out, and some of the Krauts were shouting at me.

I didn't understand what they said, so I asked, "What did you say?"

And a voice quietly said to me, "He said to go up there."

I recognized the voice of Sergeant Maxwell, who apparently was on the steps of the next house area behind me. About that time, a group of Krauts started toward me, so I walked toward them.

They took me to their positions just forward of where I was, and one of them searched me. He found the grenade launcher that I had put into my field jacket pocket after I used my last rifle grenade. He held it up over his head and excitedly said something in German.

One of the other Krauts pushed him aside and promptly hit me in the face with his rifle butt and I fell backward, where someone caught me. The one who hit me was grabbed by two others and whisked away.

No more flares were going off. They took me into a cave, dug out of the mountain right there on the front line. Someone asked in English if there were anyone still out there in front of their position.

I said, "No, they all took off."

And apparently they believed me because I found out much later that Sergeant Maxwell got back safely to report what had happened.

The cave was quite complex. Wooden bunk beds were lining the side. A table had some wooden chairs around it. It appeared they were well dug in and protected from our artillery fire.

They took my cigarettes. One of the German soldiers lit one for himself and then offered one to me, which I accepted. I waited for a light, but instead of striking a match, he took his cigarette as though he was going to hold it against mine so I could get a light. Instead of lighting my cigarette, he put his lit cigarette into my cheek and

47

burned my face. By now, I was really scared. My mouth was bleeding from being hit with the rifle butt, and now I had a burned cheek. I thought, *What next?*

They took me outside under guard and walked me to their rear about fifty yards to a bridge that crossed a rapidly running stream, and we waited in a crouched position for about five minutes. I heard the distinct sound of bullets whizzing and cracking overhead by the bridge. There were two bursts of about five or six rounds. The Krauts grabbed me by the arms, and we ran across the bridge to the other side.

In spite of the situation, I smiled to myself with the knowledge that this must be the bridge that I was firing interdiction at just a few weeks before when I was manning the .50-caliber machine gun for training purposes back at M Company positions.

They took me to an underground field hospital right there on the frontline positions. One of their medics cleaned the blood from my face and put some salve on the cigarette burn.

When we went back outside, there was a motorcycle with a sidecar and about four or five sharp-looking soldiers. I figured they must be officers the way everyone else was clicking their heels together and giving the "Heil Hitler" salute to them.

I found out later that everyone gave the salute to everyone else who outranked him, regardless of whether they were officers or not. A private saluted a PFC in that army. As a private myself, I didn't think much of the idea.

One of them tied my hands behind my back and helped me into the sidecar. One of the Krauts, armed with a Schmeisser, got on the motorcycle behind the driver. Then someone squished me down in the seat and put a canvas tarp over the top of the sidecar. We then drove several miles to a rear MP station.

When we arrived, I was untied, and the blindfold was removed. I could hardly move my arms after that long, bumpy ride. They then put me into a windowless room and left me there until early evening of 23 February. I was permitted to relieve myself at an outside portable latrine in full view of the mixed civilian population on the farm. I became so constipated that I had stomach cramps for a week before I was able to pass any solid excretion. Here they gave me my first food, a cup of hot barley juice and a mess kit of soup that I couldn't bring myself to eat.

The next morning, they took me from the MP station a little farther into the Po Valley. I was put into a room that measured about eight feet by ten feet and had about a bale of straw scattered on the floor and a filthy blanket. The place was crawling with lice.

They got me up at 0600 and gave me a cup of herb tea. I can't explain the taste of it because I never tasted anything like it before. It was awful. For dinner, I got a cup of soup, the same slop that was given to me at the MP station. Supper brought coffee and black bread. However, it looked like coffee, but I couldn't place the taste.

In between meals, I had nothing to do but think. I often thought of my folks and how they would take the MIA report that was bound to come. I thought of home and my girlfriend. When someone is in a position such as this, lots of things run through his mind. He gets to thinking deeply, and he gets more homesick and lonely than he has ever been.

I had to cheer myself up, so I started to sing. The only songs I could think of were sentimental songs. It made me more blue. I started to talk to myself but checked myself. It was quite a strain.

During the first week, I was interrogated in the headquarters where I was required to stand barefoot in a circle that was drawn on the floor in the center of the room. I was not given any rest. I was taken to the HQ about every two hours and questioned by at least three different officers, always in my bare feet on the cold concrete floor.

After a while, they got so tired of hearing my name, rank, and serial number that one of the guards in the room grabbed me by the arm and physically threw me against the concrete wall so hard that both my elbows bled and felt like they were broken. I had my hands up to protect my face, but I still got a cut over my eye.

The ironic part of this is that they thought I should know something about what was going on within my outfit. I had the shoulder patch on my field jacket, so there was no question that I was in the 88th Infantry Division. I was a private, and here they were, showing me maps of the positions they had marked with unit designations that I had no idea at the time of who was where or anything else.

After three or four days of this, they had me moved to a holding area farther in the Po Valley north of Bologna. There were about five other Americans, some Canadians, Italians, and Indians from Nepal.

On the third day, the Jerries put me in another room. There were four other PWs there. My morale went up one hundred percent. The American, David Parker, was from Virginia. The Englishman was Collins, the Canadian was Gauley, and the Indian was Kohn Maund. But we called him Jonney. He could speak a little Italian, so we were able to have a little conversation. Actually very little.

All the Indian ever did was stand at the barred window and chant. It was driving Collins mad. He took off his shoes on occasions to threaten Jonney. Parker and I sang American hillbilly songs to keep Jonney quiet, but he went on without paying attention to us. I don't know how he did it. We made such a racket that the Jerries would have to tell us to be quiet.

We were put to work chopping wood just outside the house. We did as little as we possibly could without the Germans jumping on us for not working. They paid us with four cigarettes a day. That was a big deal, believe me. I went without a cigarette for three days in the little, dark room.

The food ration per day consisted of a half cup of potato soup, one slice of sawdust-filled black bread, a pat of margarine, and a cup of warm barley juice. This ration remained constant until release on 5 May 1945.

Top: The German army used this schoolhouse in Ospitale, Italy, as a prison. The school still stands, seemingly unchanged.
Bottom: The well outside the schoolhouse. POWs sometimes received bread from Italian civilians along with water from the well.

Ospitale

The time went a little faster for me now that I had work to do and people to talk to. After seven days all told, Gauley, Jonney, and I were sent to the little town of Ospitale in the province of Ferrara.

The POW camp there was in a school building. When I arrived, an American, Charlie Graffio from Coney Island, Brooklyn, came to greet me. The Jerries appointed him camp sergeant. Charlie had food for us that he had managed to save from the day's rations. In this school building, we slept on straw mattresses mounted on wooden bunks, double decker-style.

When morning came, I was called up to the German HQ building. A German who was close to seven feet tall escorted me there. He spoke English, just like the British. He spent several years in Australia. Incidentally he was a POW in the last war, and the British in Ireland or Scotland—I don't remember which—had held him captive.

When we arrived at their headquarters, three Germans confronted me. None of them spoke English half as well as the big German who escorted me. A big, stout man named Max seemed to have a perpetual smile on his face. A corporal in the Luftwaffe was decidedly a Nazi. Finally there was a short fellow named Dick. I don't know where he got that name, but he had it nonetheless.

The German with the smile, Max, asked my name, rank, and serial number, so I told him. He asked my outfit, so I remained silent. Then he asked my home address, and to that, I answered, "Brooklyn, New York." And that was all.

Max laughed and asked if I were one of those well-known Brooklyn gangsters, so I laughed at him as if to say that he was the gangster. He didn't say anything, but his smile withered away.

He told me that he lived in Coney Island for some twenty years and bought fish from Charlie Graffio's father, who had a fish store. Charlie later told me that was correct. Max explained the rules of the camp and told me that I had to comply or suffer the consequences.

I didn't ask him what they were, as I figured that I would find out soon enough.

When I left their headquarters and was taken back to the compound, I was introduced to all the POWs. There were about twenty-two of them, seventeen of which were Canadians. They were all taken at once. One Canadian, Clayton Lightfoot, used to sing hymns for us. He was one of the swellest fellows I ever met. To me, he seemed to be more American than most of the people I knew in the United States. He was in the Royal Canadian Regiment (RCR) and was proud of it. We used to kid him by saying that the RCR was a branch of the Red Cross Reserves. He took it all in fun.

Our duties consisted of chopping wood and general cleaning in and around the school building. Aside from that, we had practically nothing else to do. As it was, we weren't fed enough substantial food even to do that work.

An SS officer inspected the quarters every morning with a German major and Camp Sergeant Charlie Graffio. The school building was two stories high and had a large "POW" painted on the roof. The back of the schoolyard had a well that was shared with the people who lived in the house behind the school. We weren't allowed to go to the well for water while any civilians were there, but sometimes it was overlooked because some of the POWs were swapping clothing for cigarettes and tobacco.

I was in the camp for a few days before Sunday came around. I wanted to thank God that I was still alive, so I wanted to go to church. The German corporal from the Luftwaffe was passing by the window so I called out to him. He came over, and I gave him a sad story. I talked him into taking me to church.

When we got to the church, the people stared at the corporal and me and began whispering among themselves. I walked in and went clear up to the front. I could see the people out of the corner of my eye, looking at me. Even the priest's eyes popped when he saw an American in his church. I couldn't understand the sermon, but the mass was conducted the same all over the world.

When we came out of the church, the corporal introduced me to a very pretty Italian girl, Sylvanna. She wore her hair in long pigtails that hung down in front of her shoulders. She gave me a holy picture and wished me luck.

Later on during the day, the corporal came around and took me out again. He took me to the town of Bondeno, about two kilometers from Ospitale. I was very much surprised when I saw Sylvanna walking toward me with a package in her hand. She gave the package, which contained tobacco and cigarette papers, to me. It was the most wonderful thing that could happen to me in such a predicament. I was speechless. I had a friend on the outside! You cannot imagine how I felt. I told the corporal to thank her for me, as I couldn't speak Italian. He did so.

We started back to camp, walking along the railroad tracks, and he told me not to mention this to anyone, or he would get into trouble. When I got back to the camp, I split the tobacco with some of my buddies. I explained what had happened and wanted to ensure that they never let on that I told them. I didn't care if the corporal got into trouble. I just wanted to keep the supply of tobacco coming in.

Two days later, Sylvanna passed by the camp and waved to me. She sent some more packages to me by way of the corporal.

I used to sit in the window on the far left of the main room, watching the people as they went by. I started to see Sylvanna two or three times a day, just walking by with a girlfriend. So I decided to have a little fun. I would hold my hands in front of my shoulders and pull my left hand down as if I were holding a pigtail and pulling it down with my head going down with it. Then I would do the same with my right hand, and my head would go down on my right side. I kept this up until the girls noticed and began to giggle. From then on, they would walk by about twice as much as they did before, and for me, it made things seem a little easier to accept.

We got a few more Americans added to our little congregation in the passing of time. Sergeant Johnson; Dick Yates of Battle Creek, Michigan; and Bill Zeits of Traverse City, Michigan, were the Yanks. Bill and I got to be best of friends. Bill also got himself a source of tobacco, but he had to pay for his. He sold a jacket through a guard and had the guard buy tobacco for him. The Jerry took his coat, but Bill didn't squawk.

In the evening when it was too early to go to sleep and too dark to see, we talked mostly about home and what we were going to do after the war was over. He told me about his wife and little girl so much that I felt that I'd known him and his family for years. Actually I've never met his wife and child. I talked so much about my girlfriend with him that he got the impression that I was married to the girl. (Personally, I wish I were. I just let him go on thinking that I was. It sort of made us even.)

The interpreter, Max, came to the school building one day and told us that an American in the hospital needed blood badly. He said it was type A, so I volunteered to give him a transfusion.

I went to the hospital with him. I was looking over the patients when one called me over. He said I looked familiar. He asked me a lot of questions before he recognized me as one of the fellows he went overseas with. As soon as he mentioned that his name was Monsey, I was able to place him. A mine had blown off his leg, and he lost a lot of blood. I told him that I would see him later, and I went into another room to give the transfusion.

I was told to lie on the operating table next to another man. I did and immediately had a strap put on my arm and a needle inserted into my left arm. I asked the fellow what outfit he was from. He answered in Italian that he didn't understand English. I was flabbergasted. I had been tricked into giving blood to an Italian who was fighting for the Jerries. I didn't care too much because I figured that life is sweet to any man. However, he died two hours later.

After the transfusion was over, I got up and walked into another room to put on my shirt. I no sooner got there before I passed out. I came to in a few minutes and was helped back to the camp. When I got there, I asked to go to the HQ to see Max. When I saw him, I bitched so much about the trick that he promised me extra food and cigarettes. I got neither.

As the weeks went by, I got to talking quite a lot with the Luftwaffe corporal. I found out that all his favors—bringing the tobacco to me and taking me out occasionally—was because he lived in the house with Sylvanna's family. It was their idea, not his. He was getting my viewpoint on the war, and he didn't agree with me. We had many arguments, which led him to tell me to shut up. It got so bad that he refused to speak to me, much less take me out.

One morning when we were just being awakened, Max came into the room, grabbed me, and took me upstairs to Charlie Graffio. He told Charlie that if I didn't stop talking against Germany, he would put me on bread and water for a week in the cellar of the school. I figured the slop we were getting was bad enough to eat without getting bread and water, so I told him I'd stop. He asked if I were sorry for what I said, and I told him no. He didn't like that a bit.

We were sent to a different camp. It was in Mantova in the central part of northern Italy. Charlie stayed behind to remain in charge of the POW camp to see that the new prisoners arrived and weren't treated too badly.

Mantova

Mantova was no picnic. There were no civilians to get tobacco from and no chance to go to church. Easter Sunday rolled around on the fourth day that I was in the new camp. The Germans got a priest from a nearby church and had him celebrate mass for the Catholic POWs. The Italian Red Cross gave us six loaves of bread for the occasion. The loaves weren't big enough to amount to much, but every little bit helped.

About five hundred POWs were in Mantova, which was more than I cared for. I wanted home, but no dice. Just wishing for things doesn't make them come true. However, the camp wasn't escape proof. Five men proved that just a few days before I got there. They bribed a guard who was later shot.

One of the men who was in the escape was a 10th Mountain Division man named Saltz. He spoke German very well, so you can draw your own conclusions. Saltz was recaptured a week later and was treated very harshly, to say the least.

I met up with a Frenchman from Paris, Jean Bergis de Courgevaux. He spoke English with a slight accent. Tutored by English nurses, he then studied English in London. He was remarkably brilliant. Together we waited and looked for opportunities to escape. We were willing to take risks, but not foolish chances.

Jean could speak German well enough to make himself understood, but he couldn't speak it well enough to pass as a German. Through Jean, we bargained with the guards. We would give the guard ten American cigarettes for a loaf of bread that was hardly fit to eat. Through the Red Cross, we got the cigarettes. The Red Cross did a wonderful job.

The Red Cross parcels were sent to us by way of Geneva. We were to get one parcel per man each week. The parcels often contained canned meat, coffee, sugar, powdered milk, toilet paper, vitamins, chocolate, and cigarettes. The Germans distributed the parcels.

We got one parcel among six men. It was usually devoured within two days, if not the same day we got it. It depended largely on our willpower. We were hungry enough to forget our willpower so the food went just as soon as it was given to us. If it weren't for the Red Cross, a lot of men would have starved.

Here's how the camp was laid out and operated. Barbed wire separated three compounds. In the large compound, there were two large garages. In one of the buildings, the Russians and the Italian prisoners were kept. In the other, all the rest of the POWs were kept. The other two compounds were empty.

Near one end of the camp, at about two hundred yards, there was a bridge. On the other end, there was a factory. Off from the third section of the square camp was the main road. To complete the square, there was a large lake. Three P-47s came over daily and dropped bombs on these targets while enemy 50s rattled away. Whenever the planes appeared, the POWs disappeared. Bullets and shrapnel flew all over the place. We had to duck our own Air Corps!

Our day started at 0630 when the Germans opened the garage doors to wake us up. We had ten minutes to get up and dressed and then get out with our mess cup for our so-called tea. If we weren't out in ten minutes, they locked the doors, and we did without breakfast. I never did, as I couldn't afford to. I couldn't afford to lose weight, so I showed up for every meal, bargained for what I could, and stole what I could from the Germans. We were desperately in need of food all the time.

After morning chow, we lined up for a count from the Germans. If there were no one missing, we went on with the usual day of the same monotonous things. If someone were missing, they called roll and locked us up for the rest of the day while they searched the premises.

At 0800, we fell out for physical training. Can you imagine? We had to jump around for an hour. It wasn't bad enough that we weren't properly fed, but to make sure that we were kept fit, the Germans made us do PT. From 0900 until noon, we did nothing. We couldn't do anything if we wanted to. We were so weak. The Germans knew that if they kept us in a weak condition, we wouldn't get very far if by chance one of us escaped.

At noon, we had a mess kit of soup. It consisted of more starch and water than anything else. From one day to the next, one could never tell what they put into the slop. Sometimes it had too much starch; other times it was too much water.

At 1300, we had another count. They weren't taking any chances. From 1330 until 1900, we did nothing but lay around thinking, hoping, and praying. We'd think of a certain sweet girl back home. Maybe she had blue eyes or brown ones. One thinks just about all the things one loves and misses. I was lonely all the time. It was no fun to go without mail from the ones you loved.

From 1900 to 0650, one schemed or plotted ways to escape or thought of home some more until one got tired enough to sleep.

A big German sergeant major, Dimmes, enforced these rules. Years ago, he lived in Chicago. He always boasted that once the war was over, he was going back to Chicago. He was always bullying the POWs.

We hoped the Yanks would start a push. We prayed that once they did, we'd all get back alive and be able to do the things we wanted most to do—anything from kissing our sweethearts again to building a house or fixing up our farms.

Escape Plans

After about three weeks in Mantova, we started to get more prisoners. They gave us the latest news. They told us that our hopes were coming through. The Tommies and Yanks had started pushing in Italy and were tearing through Italy with great force. A week later, we were told that we were being sent to Germany, but we knew it was impossible for them to get us there. Germany was near to capitulating.

We were all searched and sent to a different compound to await buses to take us off. While in the other compound, we organized a group of men to escape.

Most of them had been prisoners for over two years. Jean Bergis and I were the only ones who weren't Englishmen. When we boarded the buses, the "Escape Group" all got on the same bus. The plan was as follows: Whoever sat near the driver and the three guards were to jump them while another man would stop the bus. We would all take off in different directions for the hills. Jean and I were to stick together.

The trucks took off at nightfall, and everyone was tense, looking for an opportunity. There were about four buses to our rear and three to our front. If we took over the bus and stopped it, the Jerries in the back would also stop. Eventually the buses in our rear passed us up. We were in the rear of the column. Jean asked the Englishmen if they were ready, and they said no. It was too risky. We were angry at the damn Limeys.

We traveled until it was almost daybreak. Our planes had spotted the buses and started to dive. The buses stopped, and we got off to the side of the road and were strafed. We could see the dust being kicked up by the .50-caliber bullets. Again I was scared. It was close to the end, and I wanted to get home alive. I said a quick prayer or two, and I guess the other fellows did as well. The planes left. There were no opportunities to escape from then until daybreak.

We pulled up to a large square that big buildings surrounded. We were in Trenton. We were quartered on the fifth floor of a large building and could see the Germans doing close-order drill in the courtyard. All were fifteen or sixteen years old and very snappy. They did everything on the double. They practiced the Heil Hitler salute for over an hour until they had it done perfectly.

When nighttime closed in, we got on the buses and took off. This time, Jean had organized a group of Frenchmen to aid in the escape. We dropped the Englishmen from our plans and hoped for the best. This was our last chance.

After traveling for a few hours, I asked Jean if he were ready. He said he was not, so we didn't do anything. The two guards in the back were asleep, so I took one of their guns and again asked Jean. He said no, so I had to put the gun down. The guards woke up in the back when Jean said he was ready. I told him that I wasn't, so again we didn't do anything. Everyone on the bus was ready for anything, but we didn't get the opportunity. We pulled up when we got through the Alps and into Austria. We were at our final destination, so further plans were unnecessary.

Liberation

The Germans were still putting up the barbed wire when we arrived. We heard that our armored infantry had taken Mantova, and again our hopes went up. We knew we would be free within a few days.

At this camp, there was only one compound. Everyone was kept together. It was very crowded. We didn't have to do calisthenics in the morning though. We concentrated more on escaping, but we never got the chance.

On 2 May 1945, we had a blizzard. The snow really fell. The weather was quite different from that in the Po Valley. We had to remain wrapped up with a blanket to keep warm. We were given the same rations except that the Germans started to put noodles in the slop. All we could do was sweat out the end of the war.

On 5 May we heard the rumble of a tank. Everyone got as close to the barbed wire as the guards would permit. The tank stopped just outside the camp, and seven men entered. They were Americans from the 6th Armored Infantry of the 1st Armored Division. The oldest outfit in the Fifth Army liberated us.

This took place at 0900. It seemed that all our dreams were going to come true after all. At 1100, the 88th Infantry was passing by in trucks. I ran out the gate past the guard and stood on the road, yelling with joy. A jeep pulled up beside me. It was my company executive officer, Lieutenant Richards.

I first asked what had happened to Harry Green and the rest of the patrol after I was taken prisoner. He told me that Harry Green was wounded pretty badly and sent home after the patrol got back. He said that everyone in the fatal patrol got back safely except me. He asked how the Germans treated me, so I told him that the treatment was fair but the food was bad. He pulled out some rations and gave them to me. He wanted to take me back to the outfit, but as I was getting into the jeep, an American major came out and said I couldn't go because I was slated to go home.

Being liberated meant a lot to me. It meant hearing Sinatra and Crosby on the radio, seeing movies again, and being able to dance with my girlfriend once more. I was happy, and I don't mean maybe.

Trucks came that night to take us back to Florence. We rode all night and half the next day before we reached Verona. We piled out of the trucks and milled around. I told one of the Italian partisans that I'd give him a pack of American cigarettes for his pistol, so he agreed. I asked a Yank for the cigarettes and gave them to the Itie in exchange for the little six-shooter.

We were put into barracks that the Germans occupied about a week previously. A wall about ten feet high was around the barracks. We were to stay there for the night. We had a GI meal that really hit the spot. Steak and french fried potatoes smothered with onions and some good GI coffee was our first meal after we were liberated. When evening came, I decided I was going to town and get stinking drunk. I did just that.

I took one of my buddies, David Parker, with me. We went to the gate, but they wouldn't let us out, so we climbed over the wall. We met up with a few Italians, and they took us to their house and gave us more vino than we could drink. We got back to the barracks at midnight and found that everyone had left.

We went to the headquarters of the camp and explained the situation to the CO. He told us that if a truck didn't come back for us in the morning, he would lend us a driver and a jeep and take us to Florence. We stayed there for the night, and a truck came back for us.

Bill Zeits was on the truck, and he had a Jerry rifle for a souvenir. After traveling through the Po Valley and the Alpine Mountains, we reached Florence at about 0300. We were quartered in a building that the British also occupied. We woke up the next morning and were told that the rest of the POWs were in the Fifth Army rest camp, so we started out to meet them.

We walked down the streets looking like hell. Some of us had such a mixture of clothes on that no one could tell whether we were German, Italian, American, or whatnot. MPs stopped us many times, but when we explained the situation to them, they sent us on our way.

Once we joined the men at the rest camp, we were given enough money to buy cigarettes, candy, and beer, but no more. We just stayed there for the night when we took off by plane for Naples.

In the course of some eight hours, we landed in Naples and were taken through the town in GI trucks to the reppie deppie that was commonly known as the Block House. It resembled the E building that we were kept in for a day at Trenton. It was more or less an old castle that overlooked the sea. We could see the Isle of Capri from the Block House, but I never got the chance to make a visit there. Maybe someday I will.

When we got to Naples, we got fifty bucks handed to us, so we went to town. If we bought trinkets, we got gypped. If we bought liquor, we got gypped. We just plain got gypped.

We were in Naples for a week. The USS *West Point* was scheduled to sail, so we got put on it. It was only an eight-day run from Naples to Newport News, Virginia, but it seemed like eight weeks.

When we landed, we were immediately taken to Camp Patrick Henry in time for noon chow. We had a wonderful steak dinner served to us by German POWs.

Missing in Action (1945)

Al's unit knew he'd been captured on February 22, 1945. But without official notification from the Germans or the Red Cross, the War Department listed him as MIA and informed his family by telegram.

Al's family believed he was dead. A follow-up letter from the War Department did not change their minds.

THE BIOGRAPHY
THE REST OF THE STORY

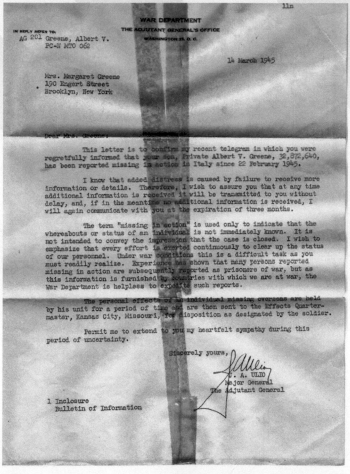

Letter from the War Department to Mrs. Greene, informing her that
Al was MIA. It is dated three weeks after Al was seen captured.

Homecoming (1945)

Upon his return from war, Al sent a telegram to his family, informing them that he had survived and was coming home. But his telegram never arrived. He reported to Fort Dix, New Jersey, where he awaited clearance for leave. Granted leave, he boarded a train from New Jersey to Greenpoint.

Carrying his duffel bag and wearing a clean, fresh uniform sporting his new rank of private first class, Al walked down Engert Avenue. The smell and sound of the city seemed like a concert in heaven compared to the muck, noise, and slop he had been accustomed to in Europe. For Albert, the war had ended, but the war in the Pacific continued.

Al climbed four steps leading to the brownstone where he remembered his parents resided. He rang the doorbell and waited. A buzzer sounded. He pushed open the heavy door at the foot of the stairs, leading to their place on the second floor. He took a deep breath, sighed, and started up the stairs.

"Do the Greenes still live here?" he yelled.

As his steps got closer to the door, he became excited and bounced up the last few steps.

Margaret opened the door, perplexed by this unexpected voice.

"Step back from the stairs," her son said. "It's your long-lost son coming home."

"Uh …" Margaret's right hand pressed her chest. Not having heard anything since the letter she received in March, she had no idea her son was home. Their apartment door swung shut, but Al placed his toe to jam it open.

"Are you real?" Margaret asked while her hands caressed Al's face.

Al led his mother to their kitchen table, placed her in her chair, and sat beside her. "Mom, I'm home." Al's quiet voice calmed her. He cradled her hands in his.

That evening, Patrick, Margaret, Kathleen, and Patrick Jr., who was also home from the war, thanked God for Albert's safe return and asked him to watch over Jimmy, who still served in the Pacific. Al was discharged from the service in December 1945.

Evelyn and Al (1946).

Postwar (1945–1946)

When Al returned home, he wanted to maintain his military training with the New York National Guard. Assigned to the 165th Infantry Regiment, the same unit in which Jimmy had served during the war, Al became an expert and trainer on the M1 rifle. He rose through the enlisted ranks and trained one weekend each month and two weeks each year.

While training at Camp Smith, Al and his buddy John took a bus just outside the gate of Camp Smith to the outskirts of Peekskill, where they walked into town.

"In June of 1946, John and I walked into Mario's Pizza Parlor there in Peekskill. Mario's was a place where we could sit and talk over pizza and meet girls," Al told me.

He looked across the room, saw two young women, and put a coin in the jukebox. "I'm going over to those girls over there. You come too. We'll ask them to dance."

"Which one you want?" John asked.

"The pretty one."

"No, I can't."

"Come on. She's not bad."

"No. I mean..." John said. "I can't dance."

Ignoring John's comment, Al guided his friend over to the table and introduced John and himself. He asked the pretty one to dance.

Evelyn May Purdy and her friend, secretaries at the Pentagon, had planned to join the civil service and work in Europe for the American occupation force. They were home on a sabbatical before returning to Washington, DC.

After a short romance, Al and Evelyn married on August 16, 1946, at the Assumption Catholic Church in Peekskill. Evelyn resigned from her position at the Pentagon.

The Albert Greene Family (1946–1953)

Newly married, Al and Evelyn lived in her parents' home on Lafayette Avenue in Peekskill, New York. They moved into the small two-room apartment attached to it, built for Evelyn's now-deceased grandmother. Evelyn's parents, Mabel and Syd Purdy, and her younger brother, Richard, also lived in the house.

Al commuted by train to Lombardy Street in Greenpoint, where he worked at Max Trunz's meat packing plant. The difficult job was hot, smelly, and boring. It was not something Al enjoyed. After discovering the process for creating different types of packaged meats, Al said, "I will not eat hot dogs or bologna ever again."

Al and Evelyn remained close to both the Greene and Purdy families. After the war, Evelyn's younger brother, Richard, joined the service. Later Richard married Lorraine Longo. They had two daughters, Kathy and Patty.

Albert and Evelyn's first child, Margaret (Peggy) Allyn Greene, was born on September 11, 1947, at Peekskill Hospital. Al moved his family in 1948 from Lafayette Avenue to an apartment in Maspeth, New York, closer to his work and to his parents in Greenpoint.

Evelyn's older brother, Robert, who had served honorably in the Navy during the war, moved upstairs on Lafayette Avenue into an apartment converted from the family's bedrooms. Robert then married Muriel Ingersol and had a daughter, Susan, just six months younger than Peggy. Their son, Sydney, was born in 1953.

The GI Bill, or Serviceman's Readjustment Act, became law in 1944. Al used this benefit to buy a small two-bedroom home in Massapequa, New York, in 1949. Beginning in 1951, he worked for Republic Aviation in Farmingdale on Long Island. As a small parts assembler at the Republic Aviation Corporation's factory, he made drop tanks for the F-84 jet fighter. To the uninitiated, these tanks looked like bombs. In fact, they carried the fuel needed during takeoff and could be jettisoned from the aircraft's wing to allow better maneuverability in combat. The jets that Al helped manufacture saw plenty of combat in Korea.

In the reserves, Al was promoted through the enlisted ranks to master sergeant. He considered enlisting full-time in the service, and after discussion with Evelyn, he enlisted into the active-duty army on March 19, 1952.

While on active duty, Al earned his high school equivalency through the GED test in July 1952. Shortly thereafter, Al's commanding officer suggested he apply for Officer's Training School. "I didn't think of myself as officer material," Al recalled later.

Master Sergeant Greene attended Officer Training School at Fort Benning, Georgia. His family returned to Peekskill to await his graduation.

After Officer Candidate School, during the last half of 1953, Second Lieutenant Greene reported for duty at Fort Leonard Wood, Missouri, for six months of training. His family joined him there. The war in Korea needed able-bodied, experienced soldiers.

After his tour at Fort Leonard Wood, he received orders for Korea, but the war ended the same month he graduated. His orders remained the same. After returning his family to Evelyn's hometown of Peekskill in New York, Al left for Korea.

First Sergeant Greene, the most senior enlisted man in
a company of about 130 men (Christmas 1952).

Lieutenant Greene relaxes in Peekskill with his family just
days before deploying to South Korea (December 1953).

Cold War (1945–1991)

After World War II, tensions rose quickly between the world's two superpowers, the United States and the USSR. Each vied for influence around the world by forming alliances, influencing or violently changing the leadership of various countries, and allying with different sides in regional conflicts. Historians say this Cold War started between 1945 and 1947 and lasted until the collapse of the USSR in 1991.

Although it was not a shooting war, millions died, and billions were spent on proxy wars. Billions more were spent as the superpowers built up their stockpiles of nuclear weapons. The world was never far from nuclear annihilation during the entire forty-five years.

Several events exacerbated relations between the United States and the USSR. In 1947, the United States implemented the Marshall Plan and spent billions on feeding and rebuilding Europe, including Germany. This increased American influence in Europe, Russia's front door.

Communism gained ground around the world. The Red Chinese kicked the American-backed nationalists out of the Chinese mainland. Seven Eastern European countries joined the Soviet Union in a military alliance called the Warsaw Pact. North Korea invaded South Korea. Soviet tanks invaded Hungary and violently reestablished communist dominance. The French army left Vietnam in defeat, and the world's great powers agreed to give the north half of Vietnam to the communists. Fidel Castro's communist guerrillas overthrew the military dictatorship in Cuba.

The proliferation of nuclear arsenals in places like the United States, the USSR, the United Kingdom, France, China, India, Pakistan, and Israel added to the tension during the time of the Cold War. People feared nuclear attack, especially after seeing the aftermath of the first atomic bombs and their radiation during World War II in Hiroshima and Nagasaki. In the 1950s, both the United States and Russia tested nuclear weapons above and below the Earth's surface.

In 1948, the Western powers distributed a new currency in Germany, the Deutsche Mark. This caused the Soviet-preferred Reichsmark to be devalued down to nothing.

In protest, the Soviets blocked ground routes into Berlin. Without food and coal, Berliners might have starved or frozen. The United States and her allies responded with a massive airlift of food and coal into Berlin for 321 days. The Soviets eventually quit their ineffective blockade, and the Germans began to appreciate the Americans even more.

The Cold War included over a hundred armed conflicts where the Soviets supported one side and the Americans supported the other. The biggest battlegrounds of the Cold War were in Korea, Vietnam, Cuba, Grenada, Afghanistan, and Angola. Many people died supporting the ideology of either America or Russia.

Korea—The 38th Parallel (1953–1954)

In June 1950, the Korean War began when tens of thousands of North Korean troops crossed south over the 38th parallel of latitude, which divided North and South Korea. Those communist forces quickly pushed the American and South Korean armies all the way back to the southernmost port of Pusan. After several years, millions had died, but neither side had defeated the other.

Under the leadership of General Douglas McArthur, the American, South Korean, and United Nations' forces regained all the land. An armistice signed in July 1953 returned the border between North and South to its original demarcation at the 38th parallel. This armistice ended the fighting, but not the hostility between these two nations. No peace treaty has been signed. North and South Korea remain at war to this day.

On February 8, 1954, Second Lieutenant Greene reported to South Korea as a platoon leader in the Thirty-Eighth Infantry Regiment attached to the Second Infantry Division.

Postwar Korea was a desolate and dangerous place. Mines littered old battlefields. The Demilitarized Zone (DMZ) on the 38th parallel dividing North from South Korea lacked even the security of barbed wire. Today, however, the DMZ is the most heavily militarized zone in the world.

Living conditions for our soldiers were austere. Most shivered in squad tents poorly warmed by kerosene heaters. Soldiers slept fully clothed with rifles nearby. North Korean soldiers could—and often did—infiltrate the South, sometimes setting up ambushes to trap "routine" patrols. There were no recreational facilities for the troops, and the local villages were often off-limits.

A story Al often told about his time in Korea shows his attitude and sense of humor:

> *I had just arrived on headquarters staff in Korea when*
> *I was told to report to the mess, so I did and sat in the*

first chair I saw. Soon all the other officers sat around me, and we commenced the meeting. Now I'm a fresh second lieutenant and a bit nervous. The general sat opposite to me. He looked at me and said, "Lieutenant, how does it feel to sit at the foot of the table?" I looked him square in the eye, smiled, and said, "Well, sir, that all depends upon the way you look at it." Meaning I was at the head and the general was at the foot. Well, the general let out a laugh, and we got along just fine.

The next time Al visited Korea—thirty-five years later—it was to visit his son, Michael, who was stationed there. Al said little about his experiences there, but he remembered the mountains, cold, and snow and mentioned his unit was tasked to respond at a moment's notice, run up a dirt road, and lay down in tactical positions ready to shoot any invading North Koreans.

As Mike drove his parents to see the modern DMZ, Al looked out over the mountainous countryside.

"Wow. That was hard," was all he said.

Second Lieutenant Greene carries a rifle in South Korea. The sign behind him has the "Rock of the Marne" crest of the 38th Infantry Regiment. The patch on Al's arm is for the "Indianhead" 2nd Infantry Division to which the 38th was attached.

Hawaii (1954–1956)

By the fall of 1954, the situation had stabilized sufficiently in Korea for the Army to return the 25th Infantry Division to its birthplace at Schofield Barracks after a twelve-year absence. The Tropic Lightning Division took on a new mission, the strategic reserve for the Pacific and the Far East.

In December, Evelyn and Peggy sailed across the Pacific with 441 other military family members on the USNS *General Simon S. Buckner*, a transport ship in use since WWII. Al met his wife and their seven-year-old daughter when they disembarked at Pearl Harbor. They settled into a small duplex off post and then moved to post housing at Schofield Barracks.

The territory of Hawaii consisted of an undeveloped group of islands in the Pacific Ocean. Pineapple and sugarcane fields dominated the island of Oahu. Soft sea breezes blew the aroma of pink plumeria, white frangipani, and yellow hibiscus everywhere. The Greenes enjoyed driving across the island, following the shoreline, stopping to swim in sparkling turquoise water, and building sand castles on white beaches.

The highlight of their stay occurred on November 15, 1955, with the birth of their son, Michael Alapaki. When explaining the meaning of Michael's middle name, Al, always a storyteller, often told this story:

> *There is a dormant volcano on the Big Island of Hawaii where you can see the most beautiful waterfall that flows down into a glistening lake called ... Well, it's called Lake Waiau. Alapaki means Alfred, the closest we could get to Albert.*

"Alapaki?" Michael said when he learned his name. "I thought I was Pōhakuloa."

Everyone called Mike *Pōhakuloa*. His nickname came from a military training area on the Big Island of Hawaii. Pōhakuloa Training Area, between the lower slopes of the dormant volcano Mauna Kea, was the training area most used by the 25th. Lieutenant Greene often trained there for four to six weeks at a time.

Evelyn and Al enjoyed Hawaii more than any other place they were stationed.

In 1956, Al received orders for Fort Devens in Massachusetts.

Al welcomes his family to Hawaii (December 1954).

The Greene family at Schofield Barracks, Hawaii, with
their new addition, Michael. First Lieutenant Greene is a
platoon leader for Company D of the 14th Infantry Regiment
attached to the 25th Infantry Division (early 1956).

Fort Devens (1956–1960)

In June 1956, the Greenes flew 2,400 miles from Hawaii to California on a four-engine propeller-driven aircraft and then drove 3,100 miles across country in a Ford without air-conditioning. The first half of the road trip, in hundred-degree heat, was on the famous Route 66, a two-lane road. No interstate highway system existed.

Al arrived at Fort Devens, Massachusetts, in July 1956. Massachusetts was certainly not exotic or temperate like Hawaii had been. Instead it had four seasons and lots of cold weather. Over four and a half years there, Al served as supply officer, special services officer, heating officer, and then commanding officer of the headquarters company.

"Keeping the camp in heat was a full-time job," he said. "I was called at all hours, like a doctor."

The Greenes lived in base housing called Devencrest. Peggy attended school first on base in a Department of Defense school and then in the little city of Ayer. Evelyn stayed at home with Michael.

Al took his family to Catholic mass on post every Sunday. They bought their groceries and clothing at the post commissary and exchange. They went ice-skating and sledding with other families and socialized at the Officer's Club every Friday evening for dinner, happy hour, bingo, and dancing. On Saturday evenings, they went to the local drive-in movie.

Thanksgiving 1958 at Fort Devens. Michael stands
beside Captain Greene, the company commander.
Al's father, Patrick, is behind him in line.

From Fort Devens, they visited various members of their extended families, who lived only from one to five hours away in Boston, Greenpoint, or Peekskill.

After his promotion to captain in 1958, Al became the commanding officer of the headquarters detachment for the garrison. His company received many awards and commendations.

Under President Eisenhower's leadership, Americans saw many improvements in transportation, education, technology, and the economy. Both civilian and military personnel realized the American dream of owning a home, having two cars in the driveway, earning a good living, and relaxing to watch television.

Television introduced Elvis Presley and brought *The Ed Sullivan Show*, *Bonanza*, and *Leave It to Beaver* into the home. Americans would watch movie stars like John Wayne, Marilyn Monroe, and Jimmy Stewart.

But not everything was good. There was a lot of fear in the fifties. The postwar Red Scare made a lasting impression on the American psyche. There were some communist spies in government, and many more were falsely accused and were ostracized, fired, or even jailed if they were suspected of being sympathetic to communism. Senator Joe McCarthy and others trampled on citizens' rights. Twenty percent of American workers were required to take a loyalty test.

The Soviet leader, Nikita Khrushchev, insisted that the world should become communist. Hungary fell to the Soviets. North and South Vietnam attacked each other. In China, the communists took over the mainland, and the American-backed nationalists retreated off the mainland to the island of Taiwan.

Closer to the United States, in October 1962, the Soviets installed nuclear missiles on the island of Cuba, just ninety miles from Florida. President Kennedy imposed a naval blockade of the island and confronted Khrushchev. The crisis ended when Kennedy agreed to remove American nuclear missiles from Turkey, near Russia's southern border. Khrushchev also pulled his missiles.

After four years at Fort Devens, Al transferred to Fort Benning, Georgia.

Fort Benning (1961)

On his way to Fort Benning's Nuclear Weapons Employment School in April 1961, Al drove his family from Massachusetts to his new station in Georgia. He decided to take a scenic route so they could visit parts of the United States they had never seen.

Racial segregation and injustice appeared everywhere during the sixties. White supremacist terror organizations like the Ku Klux Klan counted some sheriffs and politicians as members or sympathizers. Church bombings, cross burnings, and lynchings sometimes terrorized black communities.

Crossing into Alabama, Al's family saw poverty, segregation, and discrimination. This was new to them. Army posts had integrated years earlier. During a road trip in the South, the Greenes stopped at a diner. They sat at a table and looked over the menu. White people ate dinner while three black men sat separated from the other customers. A sign on the lunch counter announced plainly, but with misspellings, "Nigers not alowed."

The cook wiped his hands on his apron and said, "You niggers got to go in the back."

But the men stayed at their table. The cook pointed to the sign. The men didn't move.

A waitress came to Al's table.

"Take their order first," Al said, indicating the black men.

The waitress refused.

Al stood up and firmly announced, "If they can't eat here, we won't eat here." He walked out of the diner, leading his family to the car.

Under the influence of Martin Luther King Jr., nonviolent protests like sit-ins and marches changed public opinion and resulted in laws that called for more equality. This culminated with the passing of the Civil Rights Act of 1964.

At Fort Benning, the Greenes became friends with officers from other countries like Venezuela, Turkey, and Switzerland. They also attended the nuclear weapons school. Al's family and that of Major Hans Rapold from Switzerland often met for trips in the countryside or dinner at each other's homes.

Driving two cars, the families stopped at a Georgia lake area. Although the Greenes and Rapolds had white skin, the major's adopted daughter from India appeared black to the Southern eye. As the children played in the water, they noticed parents taking away their children. A white man talked with both Al and Hans. After a few minutes, both fathers appeared angry.

"Let's go," the two officers told their families. "We'll find somewhere else for the kids to play."

During another outing, after stopping for gasoline on a country road, the girls wanted a drink of water. They approached two water fountains; one had a sign that read "colored."

"I wonder what color that water is?" the girls asked. "Let's try it and find out." They were disappointed because the water tasted and looked the same as any other water.

The call for equal rights was not the only strain on the American people. A struggle existed between communism and democracy. There was also an escalating number of nuclear weapons. Although the United States possessed ninety percent of the twenty-five thousand nuclear warheads in the world in 1961, the American people were convinced that they were losing the Arms Race to the Soviets. The United States alone bought over seventy-seven thousand nuclear warheads during the Cold War. And they tested them. The United States and Russia exploded over 2,400 test devices in the air, in the ocean, on the ground, and even in space.

At Benning, Al completed his training for nuclear war.

First they came for the socialists, and I did not
speak out—because I was not a socialist.
Then they came for the trade unionists, and I did
not speak out—because I was not a trade
unionist.
Then they came for the Jews, and I did not speak
out—because I was not a Jew.
Then they came for me—and there was no one left
to speak for me.

Above is taken from speeches made by Pastor Martin
Niemöller (1892–1984), who commanded a U-boat during
World War I and was an outspoken nationalist after that war.
He voted for the Nazis at first but then opposed the Nazi
dictatorship and spent seven years in concentration camps.

Germany—The Wall (1961–1965)

After World War II, the victorious powers divided Germany into East and West. Russia had control of the East. America, Britain, and France controlled the West. Treaties also separated Berlin, Germany's traditional capital, into four sectors, each run by a different occupying force.

Having Berlin situated within East Germany created a problem for the Western occupiers. The Western allies could only access Berlin by several air corridors or a two-lane road with military inspection stations called Checkpoints Alpha, Bravo, and Charlie.

East Germans could immigrate to West Germany. Many simply walked away from the East and never returned. By 1961, millions had left. Most were young skilled workers. This "brain drain" weakened the East German economy and embarrassed the Soviets.

On the night of August 12–13, 1961, East German army engineers erected a barbed wire barricade encircling West Berlin. Two days later, they began building a wall to replace the fence. This prevented East Germans from reaching freedom through Berlin. Germans could no longer visit relatives or work on the other side.

The premier of the Soviet Union, Nikita Khrushchev, insisted that the American, British, and French armies leave Berlin. The Soviet army moved three divisions to the outskirts of Berlin. President Kennedy doubled the draft and ordered 148,000 guardsmen and reservists called up to active duty. The Air National Guard sent 216 fighter aircraft to Europe.

Ten Soviet T55 tanks drove to Checkpoint Charlie, where they faced American M48 tanks. But neither side wanted to go to war over Berlin. So on October 27, a Soviet tank backed up five meters. Next, an American tank backed up. The tanks left the area, and the tension was relieved.

What many people didn't know at the time was how devastating war with the communists could be. The Soviets and the Warsaw Pact forces badly outnumbered the American and NATO forces. Secretly, it was expected that the forces of the West would be overwhelmed in tank battles and the Eastern Bloc would dominate the battlefield in West Germany. The Americans, pushed back against the Rhine River, would employ tactical nuclear weapons. Al had been trained at Fort Benning for this contingency.

View from the West Berlin side of the wall.

On the western side of the wall, people protested by drawing colorful graffiti on it. The eastern side, however, was painted white, which allowed guards to see potential escapees more easily. Footprints in the fine sand alerted guards to any escape attempt. Barriers of all sorts were erected on the eastern side, including explosive land mines.

During the following twenty-eight years, 1961–1989, the Berlin Wall was reinforced with concrete, manned towers, and mines. Border guards killed hundreds of citizens trying to escape. Most of those who attempted escape were arrested and lingered in prison for years. Sometimes the guards escaped.

Captain Greene arrived in Heilbronn, Germany, in early September 1961.

American and Soviet tanks face each other at
the border of East and West Berlin.

Conrad Schumann, a nineteen-year-old East German
border guard, jumps the fence to freedom just one
day before a wall would replace the wire.

Heilbronn—Visit from Max (1961–1962)

After training at the Nuclear Weapon Employment School in Georgia, Captain Greene received orders for Germany. This was an unaccompanied assignment, so he settled his family in Peekskill, New York, before flying to Germany alone. In Peekskill, Michael started first grade, and Peggy began high school. Al reported to the Fourth Armored Division in Heilbronn during early September 1961. He became the training and security officer there.

Back in the States during Thanksgiving, Evelyn suffered a nervous breakdown. Al received permission to quickly return Stateside and pick up his family. They paid their own way to Germany and rented an apartment in Heilbronn.

Once reunited with her husband, Evelyn recovered. With the help of local residents and military spouses, the family maintained a good life on the German economy. Peggy and Michael attended a school on post run by the Department of Defense. Albert continued his duty training soldiers.

While at his desk signing the day report one day, Al heard a staccato sound similar to heavy taps on metal. Click … click … click.

Al froze, pen in midair. A white-gloved hand brushed across his desk. Al looked up from his desk, right into the face of a smiling hulk of a man.

"I never expected to see him again," Al told me. "It was Max, the guard from my POW camp during World War II." [See Al's memoir.]

Al stood, reached across his desk, and shook his old enemy's hand. During Al's several months in Max's custody, they shared many experiences. Although their memories were not pleasant, both knew the other had served his own country well.

Al did not disclose how Max found him after all those years or why. He invited Max and his wife to accompany him and Evelyn for the German-American Ball scheduled for a few weeks later.

After the visit from Max, memories of his internment and combat during World War II disturbed Al's sleep but did not interfere with his duty. Like others of the Greatest Generation, he kept those thoughts hidden in his heart. Posttraumatic stress disorder (PTSD) had not been accepted as yet.

The Greenes explored as much of Europe as possible during Al's off-duty time. Their trip to Holland during the height of the tulip season thrilled Evelyn. Along the way, they saw windmills, stopped for cheese, and watched country folk still wearing traditional Dutch attire and wooden shoes. They visited small towns, tourist attractions, and castles. In Germany, they visited Heidelberg, Rothenburg ob de Tauber, Stuttgart, and Bad Wimpfen. The center of each town displayed Maypoles and beautiful old churches.

At work in Heilbronn, Captain Greene found favor with his unit commander. Both had the same sense of priorities and values, duty, strength, and honor. But what Al didn't know would soon come to bite him. The commander, not well regarded by his superior, was soon replaced. Although new to the post, Al became caught up in this mini-purge and was told to find another post. He transferred to Crailsheim in May 1962.

Crailsheim—Visit to Ospitale (1962–1963)

At the 4th Armored Division headquarters in Crailsheim, Al served as an intelligence officer. Later he became a supply officer responsible for maintaining the unit's combat readiness through material, equipment, and supplies. But the most memorable parts of his time at Crailsheim happened while on vacation.

Always interested in history, especially World War II, foreign cultures, and geography, Al took the family sightseeing at Hitler's Eagle's Nest in Bavaria. They stayed overnight in the beautiful resort town of Berchtesgaden, once a favorite place for the Nazi elite. Then they toured Dachau.

Hitler had crammed his first concentration camp, Dachau, with thirty thousand political prisoners and foreigners captured in the countries Germany conquered. Thousands of Jews were sent there. The Greenes saw the firing range where Nazis massacred captured Soviet soldiers. They saw the massive ovens used as crematoria, the gas chambers, and a front gate at the camp entrance with a sign over it, saying, "Arbeit Macht Frei." That meant "Work Will Make You Free." This all left a lasting impression on the children.

They stopped at Salzburg in Austria, where the Greenes donned black robes and hats and slid down a wooden slide several stories underground to tour a salt mine.

The beauty of Switzerland made up for the gray skies of Germany. At Zurich, Al visited his old friend from Fort Benning, Colonel Hans Rapold, who later became a brigadier general and chief of staff of operational training in the Swiss army.

After a few days with the Rapold family and sightseeing the glorious city of Zurich, the Greenes headed south. Their old car climbed the Swiss Alps, where they stayed overnight in the thousand-year-old Saint Bernard monastery. From there, it was a quick downhill drive into Italy.

Once he entered Italy, Al's concentration changed. He became more aware of his surroundings and hypervigilant.

Evelyn held the map and navigated. "This is not the way to Rome," Evelyn said. "You need to turn back and take another street."

"All roads lead to Rome," Al remarked. "I've been here before."

Indeed he had. Twenty years before, the enemy somewhere nearby had captured him. He wasn't sure exactly where, but he followed his intuition. He slowly drove down a small road along the side of a railroad track and turned down a side street right into a small, dusty village. He parked beside a brown stucco building surrounded by fencing in the center of town. This, he explained, was the prison in which he was incarcerated during World War II. So began one of the most unforgettable experiences of his life. Al found Ospitale. [See Al's memoir.]

Not much had changed. Nazi symbol graffiti still showed through a light coat of paint that covered the old building. The townsfolk remembered their history and welcomed this returning American. Diana, the town's beautician, spoke English and translated.

When both she and Al realized they remembered each other, the mayor called for a celebration. He, along with an entourage, escorted Al and his family through the old schoolhouse turned prison, still used as a meeting hall. Although the building was clean and bare of furniture, the crap closet, window bars, and old well still existed. Al's eyes focused in the distance as he remembered and shared experiences kept hidden so long.

Standing beside the old crap closet, Al sighed as he pondered the past. "I was the youngest and smallest private in camp, so cleaning the crap out of this hole became my job."

Other prisoners lowered him down into the crap hole and sent a bucket after him. He cleaned out the excrement, sent the bucket back up, and did it all over again. A guard, often Max, escorted him to the railroad tracks where he dumped the buckets.

"I thought I'd never be rid of that smell."

Al also recalled teasing a pretty girl as she and a friend, who happened to be Diana, walked by on their way to work.

"I stood right here," Al said while moving toward the lone window covered in bars. He smiled to himself and moved his arms side to side and up and down as if pulling hair.

Even incarcerated, teenage Private Greene flirted with pretty girls. Her name was Sylvanna.

During the war, the German army commandeered everything needed to sustain their troops. A German corporal who was sweet on Sylvanna had occupied her home. She convinced him to give the handsome young man behind the window extra bread or cigarettes.

As a lifelong Catholic, Al asked a guard, who might have been Max, to take him to church so he could thank God for sparing his life.

"I walked into the village church on Sunday followed by a gun-toting guard. I walked right up to the front and sat in the first pew." Al giggled softly.

Amazed, the priest continued his service in Latin while the American soldier genuflected. After the service, Sylvanna walked up to him and handed him a box containing cigarettes and bread. After that, Al and other prisoners sometimes found a loaf of bread by the well when they retrieved their water.

Diana arranged a meeting with Sylvanna at her home in Bondeno.

Visiting Sylvanna, the woman who helped Private Greene when he was in the POW camp at Ospitale. Michael sits between Sylvanna and Al. Al's daughter, Peggy, sits across the table (1962).

For Albert, this accidental excursion into his wartime past helped heal tough memories, brought closure to his worries of what might have happened to those who helped him, and allowed him to share a difficult time with his family he would never have shared otherwise.

Time became short after this unexpected detour, so the family drove on to Pisa and Rome. As Al raced back to his post in Crailsheim, he passed by his second POW camp at Montova, but didn't stop.

"Ich Bin Ein Berliner" (1963)

In June 1963, President Kennedy visited Berlin. Surrounded by perhaps 450,000 adoring German fans, JFK gave one of his most inspirational speeches:

> *There are many people in the world who really don't understand, or say they don't, what is the great issue between the free world and the communist world. Let them come to Berlin. There are some who say that communism is the wave of the future. Let them come to Berlin. And there are even a few who say that it's true that communism is an evil system, but it permits us to make economic progress. Lasst Sie nach Berlin kommen—let them come to Berlin!*

Millions of Germans listened and were moved. Al and his friends watched the speech on a black-and-white television at the officer's club when they heard Kennedy say,

> *Freedom has many difficulties and democracy is not perfect, but we have never had to put a wall up to keep our people in, to prevent them from leaving us ... All free men, wherever they may live, are citizens of Berlin, and therefore, as a free man, I take pride in the words, "Ich bin ein Berliner."*

That inspired Al and his fellow officers as well.

"We all joined in clapping," he said. "We knew why we were there."

Bamberg—Visit with Jean Bergis
(1963–1965)

In the early summer of 1963, Captain Greene transferred to the 4th Armored Division's offices in Warner Barracks, Bamberg, Germany.

"I had completed the day's work and just headed to the school auditorium where my son was due to receive an award from his Boy Scout leader," Al said. "I sat next to my wife and daughter. We expected to see my son receive an award. Instead a soldier whispered in my ear, 'Sir, they shot the president.'"

Captain Greene immediately left the assembly, reported back to his headquarters, and readied for whatever would come. He knew what to do. After all, he had prepared for the unexpected throughout his military career. He was ready for all contingencies. The threat of possible nuclear war hung like a roiling black cloud before the thunder. Engines roared, and tanks rumbled as the 4th Armored Division vacated Bamberg for their assigned wartime positions on Germany's borders.

Families hurried to their quarters, retrieved emergency supplies, and waited for orders to evacuate. News of the assassination of President Kennedy, the oath taken by now-President Johnson, and the arrest of the assassin, Lee Harvey Oswald, all followed by the point-blank murder of Oswald by Jack Ruby, led to many conspiracy theories still unsolved today. People in the United States didn't seem to realize how close we had come to war.

After a tense several days, the men returned. There had been no action on the part of any of our old enemies. This, everyone decided, was not the time for a nuclear blast or global conflict. The Army came off alert but stayed awake.

During this time, Captain Art Elliott, his wife, and their two sons who had been stationed with Captain Greene in the past arrived. Their lives became significantly intertwined over the years to come.

Together the families watched replays of Kennedy's assassination and funeral. Mrs. Elliott's brother had been one of the escorts for the president.

Al received an unexpected phone call. After the initial surprise, he and the caller planned a meeting in the summer of 1964. Jean Bergis de Courgevaux, a former POW from World War II, who had met Al at the camp in Montova, wanted to reconnect. After twenty years, he managed to find Al. How Jean knew Al's posting remains a mystery.

Jean had amassed a fortune after the war. He and his family worked closely with French president Charles DeGaulle. Jean told Al he wanted to buy a castle in the Bordeau area of France, and he invited Al and his family to join him there.

Eager for this meeting, Al requested and was granted extra leave time, so the family traveled by car across the French-German border, stopped in Paris for a short time, and continued on to the meeting point in the south of France.

Seeing Jean again brought back many memories and emotions. They talked for hours over the course of two days, many meals, and much wine. This meeting gave them some closure, as they both relived frightening experiences, cleared up misunderstandings, and continued healing.

Twenty-year-old Private Greene had experienced anxiety, fear, pain, and humiliation during his combat service and as a POW. Twentysomething-year-old French resistance fighter Jean Bergis de Courgevaux had experienced the same misfortunes. This bond created a camaraderie that didn't break despite being an ocean apart from each other for twenty years.

Jean fought during many campaigns in the French resistance. He had been captured and imprisoned for more than a year prior to meeting Private Greene during a transfer to the POW camp at Montova. When Jean and Al were prisoners near the end of the war, the Allies moved north from the south of Italy, pushing the Germans back across their border. Germans fought the remaining months of the war within "das Vaterland." The transportation of prisoners toward Germany began, preventing the Allies from liberating POW camps. With no desire to go to Germany, Jean and Al planned an escape.

The bus transporting Jean and Al had no back window. They deduced that if the bus traveled slow enough and zigzagged within the convoy, the men could jump out of the window and run throughout the countryside to freedom.

They arranged code words. "New York" meant go; "Chicago" meant abort. The honor of that decision laid on Jean. The prisoners, mostly British, tensed at the ready. After several hours of travel, the German guard next to Al fell asleep. Al looked toward the front of the bus. An Englishman had taken the rifle of the guard who had fallen asleep next to him. Al tightened. Sweat trickled across his forehead.

Nervous as hell, Al slipped the German's rifle slowly and quietly from the guard's hands. All the prisoners watched and waited, ready to jump. Al looked toward Jean, hoping to hear him say the words, "New York."

Jean muttered, "Chicago."

Al needed to return the rifle into the guard's hands without waking him. Taking a deep breath, he pulled it off. The convoy continued, and Jean and Al remained prisoners until the end of the war.

Two decades had passed. Jean and Al were free men on French soil, watching their children play in vast fields of green. Jean turned serious and brought up the subject that had bothered each of them every day for twenty years.

"Al, do you know why I called off the escape?"

"I was mad as hell at first. Why?"

"As our bus passed around the corner of the mountain," Jean said, "the bright moon showed the shadow of the bus on the side of the mountain. You remember our bus was different from the rest. I saw the shadow of a Kraut machine gun nest on top."

Stunned, Al looked at the floor, shaking his head. "It would have been a bloodbath."

This time together helped both men come to terms with the past. By the spring of 1965, Captain Greene transferred from Germany to Fort Polk, Louisiana. The Cold War continued but focused on a land few Americans had heard of, Vietnam.

Fort Polk (1965–1967)

Al stands in the background on the left watching his son Michael
receive a Boy Scout award. Another scout leader, Captain Joel
Best, stands behind Michael. Joel would later marry Peggy.

Many men trained at Fort Polk, Louisiana, outside the small town
of Leesville. The military buildup of forces under President Johnson
increased in 1965 and reached its peak in 1968 before the war's end
in 1973.

While at Fort Polk, prior to him being sent to Vietnam, Captain
Greene served first as company commander of Company D, Second
Battalion, Fourth Training Division and later as officer in charge
of plans and logistics including supply, maintenance, services, and
transportation. As company commander, he was responsible for
training young men who were either drafted into the Army or had
voluntarily signed up knowing they might be sent to war in Vietnam.
Captain Greene's company trained as clerks and used Remington
typewriters, so he named them the "Remington Rangers."

He and Evelyn often hosted younger officers at their home for dinner and maintained an active social life. One of those officers later married Peggy, Al's daughter, who was away in college in New York state. During off-duty hours, Al supported the Boy Scout program as a troop leader.

Al bought a house in Leesville from Fertitta Brothers Construction in 1966. But when he moved his family in, the road in front had not been completed. It was a nice house, but had a mud road in front. That was unacceptable.

When Al received orders for Vietnam in 1967, he didn't want to leave his family in the mud. After many calls and no action, a group of uniformed officers with a truck and a few enlisted men arrived at his home. Al called the newspaper.

Reporters watched as these officers carried furniture and other items from the house into the truck. The headlines stated, "Builder forced officer's family out of home before being shipped to Vietnam."

During the ensuing lawsuit, the Fertittas explained they couldn't build the road during the rainy season and they couldn't build the road when it was too hot. Al laughed when he told this story.

"The judge," he said, "looked incredulous and asked, 'Are you telling me that roads can't be built in Louisiana?'"

Al won his suit against the company. Within several weeks, the company paved the road. Evelyn and Michael stayed in that house during Al's tour in Vietnam. Peggy attended college nearby at Northwestern State College, now a university, in Natchitoches, Louisiana.

Vietnam (1967–1968)

Captain Greene, carrying his duffle bag and wearing a fresh uniform, joined the ranks of hundreds of soldiers standing in lines behind printed numbers showing the order they would load into airplanes headed to Vietnam. Fort Polk, Leesville, and his family were about to become memories; Vietnam would be his reality.

One of the oldest and most experienced soldiers assembled in line that day, Al had shipped out many times and gone to war zones a couple times. The first time, to combat in World War II, had ended in personal disaster that never left his spirit untroubled. The second time, to postwar Korea, left no scars. But he knew well the fear of war, had experienced the horror, and was headed into one of the ugliest wars America had ever fought.

One of the first things Al did after arriving in May 1967 was to purchase several identical tape recorders. These desktop reel-to-reel machines with handheld microphones kept the family in touch. He also sent 8 mm black-and-white silent films back home.

In one 8 mm silent film, he and two other officers drove their jeep onto a bare strip of dirt, waved at the camera, and turned to watch chopper after chopper take off, one after the other, into the air. As dust flew and soldiers held onto their hats, one could almost hear the whop-whop-whop of the Huey's blades.

In another film, Al was dressed in swim trunks. A large fuel bladder, cut in half, served as a swimming pool. A man pulled himself out of the "pool" and pointed to a handwritten sign, "Officer's Club Swimming Hole."

In his last silent film, wearing camouflage pants and a hard battle helmet and pointing a rifle, a shirtless Al smiled and waved as he exited a secure-looking bunker covered with sandbags. You could almost hear him mouth the words, "No sweat. I love you." These films didn't tell the whole story. They never showed the misery of war.

Al lived in a primitive house called a "hooch." It was spartanly appointed with a table, a refrigerator full of beer, and a narrow metal cot. A bunker dug beside the hootch surrounded by sandbags was just a stone's throw away. The officer's latrine was beside the bunker.

Al in front of his hooch in Vietnam.

During one of many mortar attacks, the base fire truck accidentally ran over a dog, leaving its puppy homeless. Al took in the puppy and cared for it. One late February night near midnight, Al was listening to a tape of Christmas music his sister Kathleen had sent him when he heard the deafening blast of mortar rounds. Al quickly turned off his lamp and switched the audio tape machine from play to record.

The frightened puppy ran around inside the hooch. Al readied his GI-issued shotgun and spent a few seconds trying to entice the frenzied pup to follow him to the bunker. When the attack ended and the "all clear" siren sounded, Al took inventory of the damage. He saw holes throughout his hooch. He opened the refrigerator to find broken bottles all over. The officer's latrine had taken a direct hit to the toilet. The puppy was okay.

Al inadvertently sent that audio tape to his son and wife who, after listening, more fully understood the dangers Al faced. His son, then twelve years old, never forgot that recording.

On another occasion, Al recorded a tape to his daughter in college when a mortar attack occurred. Again he dove for his bunker, leaving the tape recording. The attack lasted only a few minutes before he resumed his fatherly advice. "I don't know exactly what I said, but things are hopping here, and I need to get this in the mail."

His family never told him how those tapes affected them, and he never shared anything other than a few interesting anecdotes about his Vietnam experience.

On January 30, 1968, during the Chinese New Year celebration known as Tet, tens of thousands of communist troops attacked a hundred cities, surprising the American forces. Although the North Vietnamese eventually withdrew their forces, the Tet Offensive was a psychological victory for the North.

Al worked in Tay Ninh, getting supplies out to units under fire. The American base at Nui Ba Den was under attack. Helicopters took all supplies, food, water, gasoline, ammunition, building materials, and mail up that mountain. After the war, Al said he would look at that mountain, watching fire and smoke, listening to the sound of war. "We had control of the top and the bottom, but the VC were all over the rest."

On one trip, after delivering the goods to the men, Captain Greene took custody of a young Viet Cong enemy captured in battle. Al kept his left hand firmly on the prisoner's neck. As the helicopter began to lift off, the prisoner shook visibly with fear. There had been reports that some soldiers had thrown prisoners from helicopters. Knowing the fear associated with capture, Captain Greene ensured the man's safety during transport.

While in Vietnam, Al met an old friend from Germany, Art Elliott, who had served several tours in Vietnam and was an adviser to the South Vietnamese Army. Later during the Battle of Dak Seang in 1970, most of the American advisers were killed when the North Vietnamese Army overran the Special Forces camp there. Art was wounded, captured, and forced to walk to Hanoi for two months. Then he was imprisoned for a thousand days until the end of the war in 1973. During that time, the US Army did not know if he was alive. So when the POWs were released at the end of the war, Al was surprised to see Art get off the Operation Homecoming plane. A lot of people celebrated Art's return to his family.

Major Art Elliott is the tall Texan with Al. He would be captured and held for three years (October 1967).

Mogas Aflame—Third Bronze Star (1968)

Most people run from danger. Few brave souls rise to the occasion. The motor gasoline (mogas) storage facilities for the American base at Tay Ninh, just fifty miles west of Saigon, had no pipeline, so fuel was stored in rubber bladders that stored from ten thousand to fifty thousand gallons each.

Just before dawn on April 25, 1968, Charlie opened up with mortars. Rounds landed all over the base. Deeming it too dangerous to venture out into the camp, Al stayed in his tiny makeshift bunker with a shotgun and listened for signs of a ground attack.

Then a huge explosion lit up the sky like daytime. The inside of Al's hooch lit up brightly, so he looked out the door across the dirt road to the fuel depot. One of the gasoline bladders had become a giant torch, lighting up the whole base, with flames that touched the sky. *Holy cow*, he thought. Then he remembered the warehouses full of equipment and the other fuel bladders.

These are Al's words from a tape recording he sent home the next day:

> *I was rudely awakened this morning at 0645 by our first incoming mortar rounds in twenty days. I counted fifteen, but there were actually eighteen. There were three either duds or delayed fuses ... We're not sure which. We just found them and blew them in place. Anyway, when the first mortar round went off, it was real close, and I dove into my bunker and hollered out for Major Dunn, my next-door neighbor, to get into his bunker, which he promptly did.*
>
> *When the first round went off, I was in my bunker before the second one came in. Fifteen in all, faster*

than about one per second. They were dropping all around, right close by. And I was real concerned because this is where we have all our fuel, diesel, gasoline, aviation gasoline, and stuff like this.

As soon as the last round landed and there was a break of about four seconds—of course by this time, I was pretty well dressed—I told Major Dunn, "I think they stopped coming in. I'm gonna go to the can." And I went outside.

As soon as I opened the door, I saw this billowing fire, really something I've never seen this close up, about forty yards. This raging fire and black smoke was billowing up into the air. And I yelled to Major Dunn, "We've got a fire!" So I picked up the phone and told the operator, "This is the brigade fire marshal. Call every major unit on the post and have them bring their water trucks to the fire right now!"

I hung up and ran out, and I got to the fire. We got one fire truck positioned before the last round landed. Our firefighters were out there fighting the fire while being bombed by mortars. I helped them pull out the hoses and tried to contain the fire. Working like a dog. Sweatin' like a bull.

Colonel Adams, the deputy commander, was there, so I walked over to him and reported, and he says, "Captain Greene, are you the fire marshal?" I said, "Yes, sir." And he said, "Well, why don't you put out the fire." (Laughter.) I said, "Yes, sir, but we're not going to put it out right now. We're going to contain it, keep it from spreading, and let it burn out." He said, "Carry on."

We had one ten-thousand-gallon bladder of gasoline flaming up, just raging. And it spread to the next ten-thousand-gallon gasoline storage bladder. It's all surrounded by sandbags to stop leaks. But sandbags can't stop the flames.

There was twenty thousand gallons of gasoline just raging. And the heat was something. The fire truck was mixing water with foam and spraying it through two hoses.

A fireman started yelling, "I need relief. Relief!" He was hot as a sonovagun. So I ran over and took the hose from him, and he went back to cool off.

Al ran to the hose, picked it up, and yanked it hard. It was pressurized and hard to direct. It was meant for two men to hold up while a third directed the nozzle with both hands. He tucked the hose up under his elbow and leaned forward, running toward the flames. He and the fire department fought the gasoline-fed flames together.

They have these big hoods like spaceman helmets to keep cool, and I didn't have one. So I got hot a whole lot faster than the firemen did. There were six enlisted men and myself. We relieved each other, back and forth. I got there about 0700, and at five to eight, we determined it was under control enough that I could go to the morning briefing. I was exhausted.

Captain Greene left his men with the remaining fire and reported directly for his morning briefing. His words continue:

I looked like the dickens, soaking wet. All the commanders were there and every staff officer from the post. I arrived a few minutes late. The intel officer gave his briefing, the operations officer did his thing, and the personnel chief made a brief announcement. And then it was my turn as the head of supply. I walked up there. You can imagine what I looked like, blackened, muddy, and soaking wet.

At the briefing, Al encouraged a sense of humor.

"Gentlemen," I said casually, "I'd like to mention that we had a fire this morning." And everybody burst into laughter. Everybody on post had seen the flames. It was like the whole Standard Oil Company going up in flames.

"We have to be austere with our gas usage today," I said, "because we have none left." Everybody burst out laughing again.

So I went back to my hooch, took a shower, changed clothes, and went to work.

Colonel Adams saw me and said, "Captain Greene, if you don't mind, I wish you would dress more appropriately for my briefings." He was clearly in a good mood. So I said, "Yes, sir. And if you can keep Charlie from mortaring us, I'll stay in a clean, dry uniform." We had a little chuckle.

By eight o'clock in the morning, I felt like it had been a whole day's work. Nobody got wounded. But we did lose some equipment and, of course, the gasoline. I told my sergeant to give me the names of everyone involved. And I wrote everyone up for a medal.

Three of the firefighters were supposed to rotate back to the States that morning. But they chose to come and fight this fire. Before the last round landed, an airplane landed at the field nearby. It was arriving to pick up soldiers who were going home.

They just turned around, looked at me, and said, "Captain Greene, you know I'm supposed to rotate this morning. That's my airplane!"

But they chose to stay and fight the flames even while mortars were still landing around them. I put them in for a medal for heroism. Later I heard that Major Dunn, who is in charge of the gasoline business, is putting me in for the Soldier's Medal for my activities today. I don't expect to get it, but it's nice to know I'm being put in for it.

My boss went on R&R [rest and relaxation] yesterday to Hong Kong. He had been in Saigon for six months and had volunteered to come up here to get some action. But he didn't get any action. All he got was incoming mortar rounds. When he hears about this, boy, is he ever gonna be burned up. He would have loved to do this himself. But he wasn't here last night, so I got the action instead of him. I hope he's not mad at me!

For his heroism, Al was awarded his third Bronze Star Medal, this one with a "V" device for valor.

Retirement (1969)

After his combat tour in Vietnam ended in June 1968, Al was stationed back at Fort Polk. The Army wanted all their officers to have college degrees. He continued his education, but the college courses he needed were not offered at the times he needed them. After twenty-five years of serving his country, Al retired with the rank of major in June 1969. He was forty-five years old.

"I had a good life in the Army," was all he said.

Major Greene on the day of his retirement parade.

Second Career (1969–1989)

Al, a city boy from Brooklyn, always dreamed of working on a farm. Having the rest of his life to follow his dreams, Al leased a few acres outside of Leesville from one of his lieutenants. He and his friends renovated an old home on the property, fed the chickens and horses, and plowed the land. Then Al turned the house over to a senior master sergeant with a large family. Al also formed a partnership with a friend to produce hydroponically grown tomatoes. Al, his friend, and all their sons pitched in to build greenhouses that used chemicals instead of soil. Within two years, his business failed.

In 1969, he escorted his daughter down the aisle when she married his friend, Captain Joel Best. In 1970, he moved his family from Leesville, Louisiana, to Parkville, near Kansas City, Missouri. There he attended Park College and completed a bachelor of arts in education and sociology. Al graduated in June 1973 on the same day his son, Michael, graduated from Bishop Hogan High School.

Then Al did graduate work at the University of Missouri–Kansas City, where he earned a master's degree in counseling. During this program, he and Evelyn moved to nearby Spring Hill, Kansas, where he was employed as the school's counselor. In November, Michael enlisted in the Navy, and Al, now retired, swore him into the service.

In 1978, Al and Evelyn took a vacation to Florida and decided to stay. They bought a house in Winter Park. Al took employment as a teacher at Milwee Middle School in Longwood, a short distance away.

At Milwee, Al was given the toughest kids, the disciplinary problems. He taught them and acted as a role model and counselor to his students until they could be returned to "normal" classrooms. After training soldiers for years, he had found a second calling with children who needed discipline. Al retired from this second career in 1989. He was sixty-five years old.

Senior Life (1989–2009)

Evelyn and Al decided once again to travel the world. Every year they took one cruise or another around the Caribbean or hopped on a space-available military flight to Oahu, Hawaii. They enjoyed driving across the country, visiting relatives, and flying to foreign and domestic places where their children and grandchildren lived.

Evelyn and Al also purchased several time-share condominiums where they spent two weeks each year in Branson, Missouri, and Daytona Beach, Florida. They vacationed in the Philippines, Korea, Germany, Japan, and Puerto Rico.

Al was proud to don his uniform again on several occasions. Al swore Michael into the Navy in 1973. Al swore him in again to be an officer in the Air Force in 1984. Al also swore his grandson, Brian Best, into the Marine Corps in 1994.

Brian's enlistment ceremony was a top-heavy affair. He was sworn to the military enlisted man's oath by no less than three retired officers: Captain Michael Greene, Major Albert Greene, and Brian's father, Lieutenant Colonel Joel Best.

Al was an active member in the Military Officers Association. He held office and organized conventions for the 88th Infantry Division Association and the Central Florida Chapter of the American Ex-Prisoners of War. He also lobbied the state of Florida to recognize ex-POWs with a unique automobile license plate, and he was issued the first one, number EX-POW 001. The plate and his medals are displayed at the Eisenhower Regional Recreational Center in The Villages, Florida.

Like every other American, the attack on New York, September 11, 2001, shook Al. On the day President Bush announced the War on Terrorism, Al wrote a personal letter to a friend in Washington, DC, suggesting he be permitted to serve in any capacity helping the war effort. Of course, the reply was a polite refusal. Al was seventy-seven years old.

Major Albert Greene inducts his son, Lieutenant Michael
Greene, into the Air Force (December 1984).

L-R: Retired Captain Mike Greene, retired Major Al
Greene, USMC recruit Brian Best, retired Lieutenant
Colonel Joel Best, USMC recruiter (1994).

Taps (2009)

As Al aged, his health diminished. Unrecognized mini-strokes and diabetes caused by Agent Orange had taken their toll. After a major stroke in 2003, he entered care at a nursing home in the Veterans Administration's Community Living Center down the street from his house in Winter Park. Although he received top-notch care, he died of Alzheimer's disease on August 29, 2009. He was eight-five years and two days old.

At his funeral, beautiful flowered wreathes decorated in red, white, and blue ribbon and bouquets of dark red roses, white lilies, pink carnations, and yellow daisies brightened an otherwise gloomy day. I looked upon the weathered old man wearing my dad's dress blue uniform decorated with military badges and ribbons, lying peacefully on a satin bed in a mahogany casket. "Thank you, Lord, for his life and for relieving him of his pain." God answered in thunder as rain poured.

Each time the retired military chaplain and friend who conducted the service spoke of events in my dad's life, it seemed God punctuated the talk with thunder. The last blast of thunder occurred just after my brother's final sentence in his eulogy, "Now I realize that my father didn't die. With great strength dedicated against all odds, he simply completed his life's work."

And so our family arranged for Dad's interment at Arlington National Cemetery. Major Albert Vincent Greene lies beside other warriors, fathers, husbands, and sons, whre he belongs, an unsung hero.

Peggy accepts the burial flag that had draped Al's
casket at Arlington National Cemetery (2009).

Miserable Lives of Extreme Discomfort

The Bronze Star Medal began as an infantry protest against the Air Medal that Congress had approved for fliers in the Army Air Force. General George C. Marshall wrote to President Roosevelt,

> The awards of the Air Medal has had an adverse reaction on the ground troops, particularly the Infantry riflemen who are now suffering the heaviest losses, air or ground, in the Army, and enduring the greatest hardships ... The fact that the ground troops, Infantry in particular, lead miserable lives of extreme discomfort and are the ones who must close in personal combat with the enemy, makes the maintenance of their morale of great importance.

In short order, the Bronze Star was authorized, designed, and issued.

The Prisoner of War Medal was authorized in 1985 and is retroactive back to 1917. The American eagle surrounded by barbed wire and bayonet points stands with pride and dignity, on the alert for the opportunity to seize hold of beloved freedom, symbolizing the hope that upholds the spirit of the prisoner of war.

Military Awards

During his twenty-five-year army career, Al was awarded nineteen decorations.

- Bronze Star: Three awards and a "V" device for valor
- Purple Heart: Injuries received while a prisoner of war
- Army Commendation Medal: Three awards
- Prisoner of War Medal
- Army Good Conduct Medal
- American Campaign Medal
- European-African-Middle Eastern Campaign Medal
- World War II Victory Medal
- National Defense Service Medal: Two awards
  ○ This medal did not exist during World War II.
- Korea Service Medal
- Vietnam Service Medal: Stars for three campaigns
- Armed Forces Reserve Medal: A silver "X" year device denoting over twenty years of service in the reserves
- United Nations Service Medal (Korea)
- Republic of Vietnam Campaign Medal: A year device from 1960
  ○ The ending date is missing because the South Vietnamese government ceased to exist in 1975.

Badges

- Combat Infantryman Badge: Two awards
- Expert Qualification Badge with Carbine Bar
- Sharpshooter Badge with Auto Rifle Bar

FAMILY MEMORIES

The next few pages include memories from various members of the family.

In back: Mike Greene, Peggy Best, and Keith Best.
Seated: Albert and Evelyn Greene.
In front: Joel Best and granddaughter, Kaylee.

The Man I Love

Written from the heart by Margaret Allyn Greene
Best and read to Albert Greene on August 27, 1994

When I was very young, I would play on a hill outside our apartment and wait for my love to come. Cars drove up, letting uniformed men out, but I couldn't find the man I longed to see. Worried, scared, and anxious, I peered over the hill. "There, there! That man is waving at me." I ran into the arms of my daddy. He hugged me, smiled, and held my hand while we walked into our apartment. My daddy always hugged me and held my hand, and most importantly he always came home.

Daddy was gone. He went away to some place called Korea, where he would fly in helicopters and save other soldiers. Why didn't he come home for dinner? How come he's gone so long? Mother cried, but I knew Daddy was all right. He'd come home to me because I was his little girl. Instead we had to go to him. Would he recognize me? I don't remember exactly what the man I love looks like. Has it been too long?
"Look! That man is waving at me."
The man I love picked me up and gave me a hug. He held my hand as we went home together. My daddy always comes home.

As time passed, my brother entered the scene. Would the man I love still love me? That Christmas, the baby got a playpen, a swing, and big gifts. Had I been good enough for Santa to remember? Misgivings and rivalry for Daddy's attention left me insecure. Maybe if I run away, they'd get rid of the baby, and the man I love would come find me. Daddy found me each time I ran. He hugged me. He loved me first and could never love anyone the same as he loves me. My father is the person I could always run to and find security. We would go home together.

The baby became very sick. Was it my fault? Look how worried everyone is. I'll share the man I love. Let my brother come home. There's room in the heart of the man I love for two children. My father held me tight and shared our concern for the small baby that was my brother. It's okay to give him attention. The man I love does love both my brother and me. My father taught me that there is room in one's heart to love many people. We took the baby home.

This man I love became my favorite teacher. Jitterbug, waltz, polka, and cha-cha. Music is in his shoes, and songs are in his heart. We soared around the dance floors, keeping rhythm, laughing, and having fun. At the bewitching hours, I would sleep snug in my bed at home, knowing that my daddy was in the next room sleeping with a smile because he had taught me to have fun.

As autumn becomes winter, snow falls, and rivers turn to ice. Perilous danger hazards are everywhere. The man I love helped calm my fears and helped me learn to ice-skate, toboggan, and slide down the hill. This man never pushed me to try dangerous stunts. He urged me to learn and always held my hand and helped me up when I fell. My father gave me security and held my hand as we walked home.

The man I love was going to Germany, leaving us behind. Mama, what's wrong? Don't cry. Nothing can happen to the man I love. Thanksgiving came, and Mama fell. She wouldn't get up. Everyone cried, even Grandpa. Knock on the door. It's the man I love! Look! He came home. He makes everything all right. Mama is well. We're all going to Germany together. The man I love takes care of his family. My father taught me that the family is to be protected. Papa always comes home.

Curfews for teenagers. Chaperoned by my little brother. Mad money. Car keys. No soldier dating. Homework. College. Friends. Through all the trials of adolescence, the man I love stood firm. Three-minute phone calls. No smoking. No drinking. Go to church every Sunday.

The man I love survived my adolescence and gave me strength to survive my own daughter's teen years.

College. Away from home, I remembered the lessons I learned from the man I love. Vietnam called him. I wanted to get married innumerable times. Each time Dad would send only one line, "Wait. Out." I waited until the man I love held my hand and escorted me down the aisle twenty-five years ago, giving me to the man I have learned to love.

Now the man I love is in his twilight years, surrounded by his wife, grandchildren, son, and daughter. He has shown us by example that love is always giving, sometimes taking. Love lasts through war, separation, togetherness, and sickness. Love never dies, even though the body fails. Daddy always comes home.
I love you, Dad.

The Fisherman
By Keith Best

Almost all of my memories of Grandpa involve fishing. I can't remember how many times we would go out, get a boat from the Navy base near his house, and go fishing on the hundreds of lakes and canals of Orlando. He knew all the lakes and all the canals linking the lakes.

I remember going with Grandpa to the courthouse to get his "lifetime" fishing license. Once you turn a certain age, they give you a fishing licensing for life, and you never have to pay to renew it. Anyway, we went into the courthouse and walked through the metal detectors.

Grandpa set off the metal detectors. He had this tiny can opener attached to his keys. The marshals told him he had to give it to them, and he argued with them about it. He said he had that can opener with him through two wars. He was a POW, he had that can opener with him the whole time, and he was not going to give it up to go into a government office of his country, especially since it was a can opener that had been given to him by the government in the first place. Finally they allowed him to seal it in an envelope and leave his keys with them while we went in and got his license.

P-38 can opener on a chain with dog tags.

Another time, I remember going fishing with Grandpa. We went to the naval base and checked out a boat to go fishing on the lakes, and this time, we just launched it there at the base. Well, we were drifting around the lake and fishing. There was some noise, but it was a naval base, so we ignored it. The noise got louder as we drifted across the lake. Finally we realized it was the MPs yelling at us over loudspeakers because we had drifted into restricted waters, and the nice house we were looking at was the base commander's house. We decided to move to the other side of the lake and continue fishing.

I remember Grandpa letting me drive the boat while he was sitting in the front. I later learned that, by sitting in the front of the boat, he was keeping it from getting up on plane and thereby keeping me from going too fast.

All of my best memories of Grandpa are fishing memories. I don't remember ever catching or even seeing a fish. But I remember going out on the boat, he and I, and fishing.

Grandpa was a husband, father, soldier, POW, and war hero, but I knew him as an awesome fisherman. I miss fishing with my grandpa.

The Patriot
By Brian Best

I did not know Al Greene. I knew a man named Grandpa Greene. He was an educator, a teacher of geography to be more specific. He was a patriotic man who hung the Stars and Stripes on his front porch every morning and removed it every evening at dusk. Grandpa lived in Orlando in the vicinity of the naval basic training facility.

I remember as a young boy going to a boot camp graduation ceremony and parade on the base. I remember feeling awe as the smartly dressed sailor at the gate came to rigid attention and saluted my grandfather. Standing next to him in the bleachers, I could sense the respect he had for these newly made sailors, men who had volunteered to serve the nation just as he had done, so many times before.

I didn't know then the extent of my grandfather's service and wouldn't understand the depth of his sacrifice until my own short service in the Marines. One of the proudest days of my life was the day I was sworn into the Marines. I can only imagine what my recruiter felt as he stood next to my father (Lieutenant Colonel, US Army, retired), my grandfather (Major, US Army, retired), and my uncle (Captain, US Air Force, retired), as they all swore me into the Marines. I felt a great sense of accomplishment and joy as I realized how proud my grandfather and father were.

Throughout my time in the Marines, whenever I came upon a hardship or challenge, a quick call home would often set me right. I cannot even imagine the despair and hopelessness someone would feel not being able to talk to one's family, let alone doing it while starving and locked away in a POW camp.

I knew my family was proud of me during my time in the Marines because various members of my family would show up in the strangest places and at the most unlikely times. One such occasion was when my unit had traveled to an army base in Virginia to practice tank gunnery and participate in cross-service training. We were deep in the areas of the base—off-limits to most people due to the live-fire exercise taking place and the fact that we didn't want the capabilities of our tanks to become known to our enemies. My tank was getting ready to go downrange for our combat run when we were ordered off the line and I was told to report to the CO in the range tower.

Upon reporting, my CO demanded to know who Major Greene was and what business he had with me. I was stunned and worried that something might have happened and managed to stammer out he was my grandfather. It was his turn to be stunned and speechless. All he could manage was to order me back to base camp.

As I was walking away from the tower, my grandfather's Ford came pulling up through the mud, in between the tanks and Humvees. I was an instant target of ribbing and jokes until I told my fellow marines my grandfather's story. Not another word was said. It did become a running joke, though, whenever and wherever we deployed, to guess which one of my high-ranking family members would show up. I loved it.

My last memory relating to my grandfather—and the one that fills me with great pride—is when we laid him to rest in Arlington. He had passed on some time before, so the pain of his death had faded. I walked among the gravestones, reading the names of the great and heroic Americans laid to rest there, men who had given their lives for this country. I realized the true depth of his patriotism. He had volunteered for combat in World War II, was captured and held as a POW until the war's end, and answered the call of duty in the Korean conflict and Vietnam. I take great pride in knowing that he rests with others whose patriotism matches his own.

Marine Corporal Brian Best on his M1A1 Abrams main
battle tank at Camp Lejeune, South Carolina.

Eulogy for Major Albert V. Greene
Delivered September 5, 2009, by his son, Michael

Albert Greene lived in a world forged by heroes and hard workers. Born in Greenpoint, Brooklyn, and raised in the Great Depression, he once told me "we didn't know we were poor." They just had fun playing stickball in the New York City streets until the world's biggest war called him.

He was the youngest of the Greatest Generation, the breed that built America out of the global Great Depression. He spent his formative years surrounded by the determined ones who won the most devastating war the world has ever known. He was then the youngest soldier on the battlefield. Captured, the young man suffered as no one should.

He didn't speak of it, except once he let slip that the experience haunted him every morning and every night for the rest of his life until he finally found peace with God today.

Once, while sitting quietly grading papers, he overheard someone say, "Everyone should have to suffer a bit. It builds character," which is a common belief. He suddenly nearly leapt out of his chair and firmly stated. "No, they don't." It was clear he believed in kindness, that no one had to suffer. He spent his later years ensuring those around him lived in peace.

In fact, in Vietnam, he once escorted a young Viet Cong who was captured. My father told me he ensured that the young man was not harmed while in his custody.

Intelligent but not overly intellectual, he enjoyed collecting stamps and filling his office with stamps from countries he visited and the countries he would no doubt visit today if he could.

In his seventies, he took up computers, which are not easy to figure out, because he enjoyed solving puzzles. He never gave up. He told me once that he quit every job he ever had. Indeed he quit high school. But he ended up with a master's degree. He told me he moved from factory job to factory job. Would you say he was drifting? He started as a private and ended twenty-five years later as an army commander. He taught us a lesson. If what you're doing doesn't feel right, stop! It turns out he was just finding his perfect fit.

After lifelong service in the military, he counseled and taught children. The school gave him the toughest kids, the unruly ones who disrupted other classrooms. Simply by his quiet and steady presence and his leadership in the class, he gave these special kids a sense of responsibility and discipline before returning them to normal classrooms.

Retiring for the second time, he took his wife on vacations around the world.

Through his example, my father taught me the purpose of a man was threefold: to provide for and to protect his wife, to teach his children, and to defend his country.

Did he *want* to fight wars? Once he and I were watching a war movie. There were lots of them. He was so quietly grading papers that I thought he wasn't watching. At some point in the movie, a famous character compared the smell of napalm to the feeling of victory and voiced regret that the war might soon be over. This time, my father did indeed jump out of his chair and nearly shouted his disagreement with words that cannot be repeated here. Clearly, there was no glory in war.

Why then did he stay in the service of his country for three decades? The answer, like a parable, comes in story form. Call it the parable of the fishermen and the stingray.

He enjoyed the camaraderie of his fellow officers and enlisted men. I'll never forget when I was a child he took me into the Gulf of Mexico on a large overnight fishing boat, where we netted shrimp all day to gather bait for the next morning. At night, when I was pretending to sleep in the cabin and he and the men were making lots of noise topside, the cabin door suddenly blew open, and the largest stingray known by man to inhabit the ocean flopped across the deck, swishing its deadly tail all about. Dad simply picked the monster up and threw it overboard, ignoring the danger and saving the day.

Was he courageous or foolish? Once he told me how, in a nighttime mortar attack, he sat on the hood of a jeep with a flashlight in one hand as they drove along slowly, looking for unexploded bombs on the runway. Somebody had to do it.

You see, he had discovered early in life that he could carry the cross. Having learned of fortitude and inner strength early on, he continued to sacrifice himself so that others would not have to suffer. Maybe that's why he was religious. Jesus and my father were all about sacrifice.

He was also laughing all the time, but quietly, inside. With his intelligence and experience, he easily saw contradictions and juxtapositions that others never noticed. So he often would simply look at the world around him and smile knowingly, kind of giggling to himself.

In his last days, he returned to being surrounded by veterans, where his life began. Once, while he was in intensive care, I noticed the VA had given him a simple smock to wear, which said, "Property of US Government. Not for Sale." I think he would have looked at that smock and laughed with the sentiment. Considering his lifelong service to his country and his steadfast refusal to compromise on values, he was indeed government property and definitely not for sale.

His last trip to the intensive care unit was quite traumatic. I've never seen nor heard of a human being fighting for breath so hard for so many hours and days! Any normal man would have given up and died of exhaustion. But he continued to hang on for a week after his doctors said he should have died, until his family could join him, until we each had visited, until every one of us could say goodbye. I believe he was deliberately bringing his family together.

Now I realize that my father didn't die. With great strength dedicated against all odds, he simply completed his life's work.

POEMS FROM A POW CAMP

Al carried the following two poems written on scraps of paper, one of which was the brown, stiff toilet paper prisoners used, through several different POW camps. Upon returning home, he gave them to his sister, Kathleen.

The Last of My Battle Days ★

*Composed by Albert V. Greene
when a prisoner of the Germans
during World War II*

Just that one February night, I hate.
But now I know it is too late.
All I can do right now is pray
That the fellows got away.

There, next to me, was a pool of red.
I knew right then that the sergeant was dead.
My ammo was gone; it really was tough.
And boy, those damn Jerries sure treated me rough.

One stood right there with a burp gun in hand.
Seeing this, the other two ran.
I grabbed at his gun and threw him to the ground.
He gave out a yell that turned the other two 'round.

They came back again, looking much bolder.
Both grabbed my arms close to my shoulder.
They dragged me downhill; I thought I would die.
They thought I was wounded, and so did I.

There were holes in my jacket, pants, and my hat.
But no holes in me, thank God for that.
I was sent to a camp where there was no law.
It was called a camp for "Prisoners of War."

★ A Soldier's Thought ★

Written by Albert V. Greene
while a prisoner of war of the Germans in 1944

I know I've been gone for quite a while.
The war has taken away my smile.
Life has not been kind to me.
Just look at me, and you will see.

My face grows thin; my skin is light.
You'll know that I've been in the fight.
My arms and legs are skin and bone.
That's why I'm dreading coming home.

I know that you will take my hand
And say, "Yes, dear. I understand."
Then you'll say, "I still love you."
I wonder, though, if you really do.

I know, my dear, that things won't be
Just the same for you and me.
You won't love me as you did before.
That's why I curse this great world war.

I wonder though, had I stayed behind,
Would you think me as a swine?
Or would you say that it's only right
That I should get into the fight?

Whichever it is, it's too late now.
I wish that I could tell you how
Each of our little battles was fought.
But it must remain in a soldier's thought.

WORLD WAR II GLOSSARY

1A: Eligible for unlimited military service. A military draft classification.

10-in-1 ration: A package of meals that could feed ten men.

50s and 60s: Heavy machine guns.

88: The best gun of the war. The German 88 mm cannon could destroy aircraft or tanks.

AWOL: Absent without leave.

AUS: Army of the United States. Draftees had shorter enlistments and different promotion plans than volunteers, who were Regular Army (RA, not AUS). This organization scheme was also used during the Korean and Vietnam wars.

artillery: Cannon.

B-bag: A cloth barracks bag used to store and transport personal clothing.

Blue Devils: The Eighty-Eighth Infantry Division.

Bronze Star: Medal for bravery in combat.

BAR: Browning Automatic Rifle. An American light machine gun. (Pronounce each letter, B-A-R.)

burp gun: A German MP38 or MP40 submachine gun.

C-ration: Canned meals.

C-47: Military transport plane.

CO: Commanding Officer.

company: Two or more platoons, about 130–150 soldiers.

court martial: Military court of law.

Dieppe: The Allied invasion of Dieppe, France, in 1942, was a terrible loss. Most of the six thousand invaders (including five thousand Canadians) were captured, killed, or wounded.

dogface: American foot soldier serving in the infantry.

foxhole: Hole dug in the ground to protect one or two soldiers.

furlough: Vacation or leave.

GI: Government issue. Soldiers are GIs.

Great War: The Great War is now called World War I. President Wilson called it "the war to end all wars" before we knew we had to number them.

HQ: Headquarters.

Itie: Slang for Italian.

Jerry: Slang for German.

K-ration: Dehydrated emergency food.

KP: Kitchen police. Clean up.

Kraut: Slang for German.

LST: Landing Ship, Tank. Ships designed to pull up close to shore and deliver trucks and tanks and troops. Over a thousand were built.

Liberty ship: Over 2,700 cargo ships were built quickly and called Liberty ships. Average time for construction was forty-two days. Unfortunately a defective design, poor-quality steel, and a poorly trained workforce resulted in major defects. Several of the ships simply broke in two, but some sailed for over fifty years.

Limey: Slang for British.

Luftwaffe: The German air force.

MIA: Missing in Action.

MP: Military police.

Nazi: National Socialist party.

Normandy: A region on the west coast of France, the site of the D-Day landings on June 6, 1944. On the first day, 156,000 men crossed the English Channel in 7,000 vessels from eight navies, supported by 12,000 aircraft. German troops heavily defended the beaches, and 4,400 Allied troops died on the first day. "Omaha" was the code name of the beach on which most of the casualties died.

OP: Observation post.

P-47: Primarily a "pursuit" fighter aircraft, the P-47 also bombed and strafed ground targets.

PX: Post exchange. Shopping facility hosted by the US Army, where soldiers could buy American consumer goods.

potato masher: German Model 24 hand grenade.

POW: Prisoner of war.

PFC: Private first class. A very low rank.

regiment: A group of several battalions, each of which consisted of several companies. A regiment had about 1,000 men under the command of a colonel.

reppie deppie: Replacement depot. Incoming soldiers were assigned to replace outgoing or killed soldiers.

RCR: Royal Canadian Regiment.

Schmeisser: The MP40—or Maschinenpistole 40—was a favorite submachine gun of the German army. American soldiers erroneously called it a Schmeisser, believing legendary arms designer Hugo Schmeisser made it. The Erfurter Maschinenfabrik made it. Also called a burp gun.

SS: Schutzstaffel. Protection squad. Originally meant to provide protection for high-level Nazi officials, the SS grew into a million-man elite army, wearing black uniforms and entrusted with carrying out the "Final Solution" war crimes, which killed millions of civilians, including 6 million Jews.

screaming meemie: A German multiple rocket launcher, known for its terrifying sound as the rockets fly toward their targets.

shelter half: Each infantryman carried one half of a tent that could be used alone or connected to another man's shelter half, forming a simple tent.

shoe mine: The German antipersonnel Schu [shoe] mine was a simple box with 200 grams (less than half a pound) of explosive. Being made of wood, it was nearly impossible to detect.

Silver Star: A very high medal for bravery in combat.

SP: Self-propelled artillery is equipped with its own propulsion system.

Tommy: Slang for British.

Tommy gun: Popular American submachine gun.

trench foot: Serious medical condition that develops from prolonged exposure to cold and wet conditions. It could lead to the foot being amputated.

USS *West Point*: Originally a luxury liner named SS *America* and the flagship of the United States Lines. She was turned over to the Navy in 1941 to carry seven thousand servicemen per trip. In all, 350,000 soldiers sailed aboard her. She was returned to civilian service after Operation Magic Carpet, the massive return of 7 million soldiers at the end of the war.

WAC: Women's Army Corps. Female soldiers. Thousands of women served in the United States and overseas as telephone and radio operators, map analysts, camera repair technicians, and mechanics.

Yank: Slang for American.

DECODING MILITARY TIME

The American military has a unique system of notation for time. This helps with planning and coordinating operations around the world. The world is divided into twenty-four zones labeled A to Z, with J (Juliet) standing for "local" time and Z (Zulu) standing for Greenwich Mean Time (at the Royal Observatory in Greenwich, England).

The day is divided into twenty-four hours (of course), beginning with one minute after midnight, represented as 0001. So:

0100 = 1:00 a.m.	1300 = 1:00 p.m.
0200 = 2:00 a.m.	1400 = 2:00 p.m.
0300 = 3:00 a.m.	1500 = 3:00 p.m.
0400 = 4:00 a.m.	1600 = 4:00 p.m.
0500 = 5:00 a.m.	1700 = 5:00 p.m.
0600 = 6:00 a.m.	1800 = 6:00 p.m.
0700 = 7:00 a.m.	1900 = 7:00 p.m.
0800 = 8:00 a.m.	2000 = 8:00 p.m.
0900 = 9:00 a.m.	2100 = 9:00 p.m.
1000 = 10:00 a.m.	2200 = 10:00 p.m.
1100 = 11:00 a.m.	2300 = 11:00 p.m.
1200 = noon	2400 = midnight

For example, a naval war planner might decide that an attack against an enemy in the Paracel Islands should kick off in the South China Sea (H) at three in the morning. That's 0300H, or "oh three hundred Hotel." Military commanders around the world could easily convert this to their own local time. For instance, 0300H in the South China Sea would be 1900Z in England and 0900W at our Pacific headquarters in Hawaii.

ABOUT THE AUTHORS

 Albert Vincent Greene (1924–2009) served honorably in World War II, Korea, Vietnam, Germany, and the United States from 1943 to 1969. As a private first class in World War II, he was captured and held as a POW by the German Wehrmacht. He wrote the memoir included in this book to chronicle his experiences for us.

Margaret Allyn Greene Best is a retired elementary school teacher and writer. She has published in several magazines. An amateur genealogist, she has kept a journal all her life. Margaret is married and has three children and eight grandchildren. She and her husband live in The Villages, Florida. This is her first book.

 Michael Alapaki Greene is a retired military officer. In fact, he calls the *Stars and Stripes* his hometown newspaper. After the service, he published and edited a hobby magazine called *Robot Science and Technology*. He has two children and lives in Winter Park, Florida. This is his first book.